# Marine
# Birds and Mammals
# of Puget Sound

# Marine Birds and Mammals of Puget Sound

Tony Angell and Kenneth C. Balcomb III

Drawings by Tony Angell

With a Foreword by Paul Ehrlich

A Washington Sea Grant Publication
Distributed by the University of Washington Press
Seattle and London

First Published in 1982 by the
Washington Sea Grant Program
University of Washington
Second printing 1984.

Distributed by the
University of Washington Press
Seattle, Washington 98195

Publication of this book was supported by grants
(04-5-158-48; 04-7-158-44021; NA79AA-D-00054; and
NA81AA-D-00030) from the National Oceanic and
Atmospheric Administration and by funds from the
Environmental Protection Agency. Writing and
publication was conducted by the Washington Sea
Grant Program under project A/PC-7.

**Library of Congress Cataloging in Publication Data**

Angell, Tony.
  Marine birds and mammals of Puget Sound.

  Bibliography: p.
  1.  Sea birds—Washington (State)—Puget Sound.
2.  Marine mammals—Washington (State)—Puget Sound.
I.  Balcomb, Kenneth C., 1940-          II.  Title.
QL684.W2A53   1982        598.29797'7        82-10946
ISBN 0-295-95942-8

*Osprey with catch*

To my parents and children in hopes
that our book may provide a bridge of understanding
leading to a brighter future.

Tony Angell

To our wonderful neighbors,
the marine mammals of Puget Sound.

Kenneth C. Balcomb III

# Contents

 **PUGET SOUND BOOKS**

Funds to support the publication of the
Puget Sounds Books were provided by the National
Oceanic and Atmospheric Administration (NOAA)
and by the Environmental Protection Agency (EPA).

# About the Puget Sound Books

This book is one of a series of books that have been commissioned to provide readers with useful information about Puget Sound . . .

**About its physical properties**—the shape and form of the Sound, the physical and chemical nature of its waters, and the interaction of these waters with the surrounding shorelines.

**About the biological aspects** of the Sound—the plankton that form the basis of its food chains; the fishes that swim in this inland sea; the region's marine birds and mammals; and the habitats that nourish and protect its wildlife.

**About man's uses of the Sound**—his harvests of finfish, shellfish, and even seaweed; the transport of people and goods on these crowded waters; and the pursuit of recreation and esthetic fulfillment in this marine setting.

**About man and his relationships to this region**—the characteristics of the populations which surround Puget Sound; the governance of man's activities and the management of the region's natural resources; and finally, the historical uses of this magnificent resource—Puget Sound.

To produce these books has required more than five years and the dedicated efforts of more than one hundred people. This series was initiated in 1977 through a survey of several hundred potential readers with diverse and wide-ranging interests.

The collective preferences of these individuals became the standards against which the project staff and the editorial board determined the scope of each volume and decided upon the style and kind of presentation appropriate for the series.

In the Spring of 1978, a prospectus outlining these criteria and inviting expressions of interest in writing any one of the volumes was distributed to individuals, institutions, and organizations throughout Western Washington. The responses were gratifying. For each volume no fewer than two and as many as eight outlines were submitted for consideration by the staff and the editorial board. The authors who were subsequently chosen were selected not only for their expertise in a particular field but also for their ability to convey information in the manner requested.

Nevertheless, each book has a distinct flavor—the result of each author's style and demands of the subject being written about. Although each volume is part of a series, there has been little desire on the part of the staff to eliminate the individuality of each volume. Indeed, creative yet responsible expression has been encouraged.

This series would not have been undertaken without the substantial support of the Puget Sound Marine EcoSystems Analysis (MESA) Project within the Office of Marine Pollution Assessment of the National Oceanic and Atmospheric Administration. From the start, the representatives of this office have supported the conceptual design of this series, the writing, and the production. Financial support for the project was also received from the Environmental Protection Agency and from the Washington Sea Grant Program. All these agencies have supported the series as part of their continuing efforts to provide information that is useful in assessing existing and potential environmental problems, stresses, and uses of Puget Sound.

Any major undertaking such as this series requires the efforts of a great many people. Only the names of those whose closely associated with the Puget Sound Books—the writers, the editors, the illustrators and cartographers, the editorial board, the project's administrators and its sponsors—have been listed here. All these people—and many more—have contributed to this series which is dedicated to the people who live, work, and play on and beside Puget Sound.

Alyn Duxbury and Patricia Peyton
July 1982

# Foreword

I believe there are three basic reasons for not forcing to extinction our fellow creatures on Earth. One is that we have an ethical responsibility to preserve the endlessly beautiful and interesting products of a magnificent, multi-million-year evolutionary process. The second is that other species provide humanity with enormously valuable and irreplaceable direct economic benefits. The third, and perhaps most important, is that plants, animals, and microorganisms are the working parts of the ecological systems that support our society. For example, they maintain the quality of the atmosphere, ameliorate the weather, generate and preserve the soils essential to agriculture, provide nutrients to crops, recycle wastes, control the vast majority of potential agricultural pests and carriers of disease to human beings, supply food from the sea, and maintain a germ plasm "bank"that is essential to the continuance of high-yield agriculture. In short, causing the current epidemic of extinctions, civilization is sawing off the limb on which it is perched.

Extinctions of species and genetically distinct populations have now truly become epidemic. Species are now disappearing at something like 100 times the "normal" rate, and populations at a rate that may be 100 times higher than that. Most of this loss is not caused by overexploitation of prominent species such as whales and rhinos, but by destruction of habitat. That is why books such as *Marine Birds and Mammals of Puget Sound* are so important.

It is a sad fact that for most parts of the United States (and for much of the rest of the world) we don't know what organisms are where, and what habitats are critical. Now this problem has been solved for two important groups of organisms in the Puget Sound area—and none too soon. Two of the fastest growing counties in the United States border on the Sound, and demands to "develop" (read "destroy") much of the area are increasingly heard. But with the existence of this book, decision makers will no longer have the excuse that they "didn't know" what species is where or what habitats are essential for their maintenance.

But *Marine Birds and Mammals of Puget Sound* will do more than provide a valuable tool for environmentalists, planners, and responsible politicians. With its beautiful illustrations, it should help to educate the public about why it is crucial that the needs of other organisms be a prime concern in the treatment of the greater Puget Sound environment. If only we had similar works for all of the ecologically sensitive areas of our globe!

Paul R. Ehrlich

*Golden plovers over the
Strait of Juan de Fuca*

# Preface

As this book was being completed the people of Puget Sound witnessed some dramatic decisions regarding the future of the region. The Weyerhaeuser Company was securing approval for a major port facility within the last comparatively pristine estuary on southern Puget Sound at Dupont. Recently, Governor John Spellman halted plans for a docking facility in northern Puget Sound and an oil pipeline beneath its waters. With increasing demands for space and other resources one can only anticipate more proposals that would inevitably alter the existing natural network and affect the populations of marine birds and mammals. Will we be prepared to weigh the immediate benefits of development against the possible long-term losses?

Puget Sound is a region that has an incomparable wealth of marine life, which touches the aesthetic sense of humankind. Simultaneously, it hosts a large, culturally rich, and economically enterprising settlement of people. Our time here has impressed upon us that the waters and shores are far more than an assortment of species in varying numbers with particular habitat requirements. We have a living system and like necessary appendages or vital organs, the species all function in its health. The pull of one sets the others in motion. Indeed, the relative health and vitality of the Puget Sound system has not been overlooked by scientists who recently recommended that portions of Puget Sound be designated as nearshore marine sanctuaries for the East Pacific (Environmental Outlook, 1982). The areas under consideration include the San Juan Islands and Skagit Bay, waters adjacent to Dungeness Spit, Sequim Bay, the waters surrounding Protection Island, the Nisqually Delta, and the shallow waters along Anderson, McNeil, and Gertrude Islands.

To the degree that we understand the dynamics of this marine system and struggle to work within them our lives become infinitely richer. May this book serve in some way to help meet this challenge.

Tony Angell
Kenneth C. Balcomb III

July 1982

*Cassin's auklet feeding young in burrow*

# Acknowledgments

The senior author wishes to express thanks to Dennis Paulson who carefully reviewed the first draft of the marine bird section of this book. His constructive comments led to a correction of oversights, a broadening of narrative and a fuller consideration of these remarkable species. Like Paulson, the work and insights of Terry Wahl were of great importance in the compilation of information on marine birds. These two gentlemen are surely among the most knowledgeable researchers who choose to pursue studies of these families of birds.

The cooperation of the Washington State Department of Game, the Department of Ecology, and Fish and Wildlife Service is greatly appreciated. Like the aforementioned, the offices of the National Oceanic and Atmospheric Administration were very helpful in forwarding research information that was important to the completion of this work.

As our work was being completed, the new American Ornithological Union checklist was released and the latest scientific names were incorporated into the manuscript. In the general family framework, however, we have retained the approach utilized by Robbins et al. for *Birds of North America.*

Of particular importance to the development of the drawings of this book was access to museum skins that would permit the checking of details relating to plumage pattern and structure. John Rozdilski, Sue Hills, Emily Davies, and Sievert Rowher were very helpful and patient as this important part of our book was completed. Thanks, too, to Phil Mattocks of Seattle Audubon, and Peter Gellatly.

Finally, thanks to close friends and family. Dave Munsell, Barbara Morrow, Karl Kenyon, Victor Scheffer, Bill and Marty Holm, Tony Fleck, Doris Krogstrad, Paul Ehrlich, and Gordon Orians, all of whom provided either encouragement, assistance or insight on the task of completing the book. And to my wife Noel and to Bryony and Gilia, my greatest thanks for the patience and support you gave. The challenge of completing this book could only have been achieved in the creative and adventuresome atmosphere you provided.

Tony Angell

I would like to thank Dale W. Rice and staff members of the National Marine Mammal Laboratory in Seattle for their willingness to share at any time their vast collective knowledge of marine mammals. I would also like to thank Andrea Jarvela, Kirk Johnson, and the entire staff of the Washington Sea Grant office for their patient assembling and editing of bits and pieces of this manuscript mailed from the far corners of the globe as I pursued my life's work, the study of living whales at sea.

Kenneth C. Balcomb III

# Marine
# Birds and Mammals
# of Puget Sound

# A Wildlife Heritage

The Strait of Juan de Fuca, the waters surrounding the San Juan Islands, Hood Canal, and Puget Sound comprise an extraordinary inland reach of the Pacific Ocean. The formation of these waterways was largely the result of the periodic presence of glaciers over the past three million years. Tongues of ice, draped over the top of the continent, gouged, quarried, and scoured chasms along the flanks of what are now the Olympic and Cascade Mountain ranges. One glacial thrust reached some 80 miles southward from the northeast corner of the Olympic Mountains, nearly bisecting a large portion of what is today Western Washington. The ice was, at times, almost 4,000 feet thick, and as it retreated the valleys that remained were filled by the invading sea.

After the glaciers receded, shorelines were slowly shaped by the eroding forces of tide and wind, and the undersea valleys filled by sediments deposited by rivers and shifted by currents. Today, the region comprises more than 2,100 miles of inland shoreline, and although sediment has gradually filled the sea basins, some depths still exceed 600 feet. Ten major and 14 minor rivers—along with countless streams, creeks, and springs—flow into this marine system. These arteries drain nutrients from far into the interior and pump them into Puget Sound.

Along the edges, where land joins sea and freshwater rivers flow into saltwater bays, exist some of the most biologically productive habitats on earth. At the mouths of rivers, estuaries nurture specialized species. Adjoining shores of rock, sand, or mud sustain distinct communities of marine life. Here populations of marine mammals, birds, and fish come to rest, breed, and feed.

The abundance of marine life and the ease with which it could be harvested enabled the earliest inhabitants of the region to establish rich and enduring cultures. The Nootka of Vancouver Island and their neighbors to the south—the Makah, Quileute, Quinault, Clallam, and Chemacum of the Olympic Peninsula—fished and hunted whales and pinnipeds along the coasts and waterways of the Pacific Northwest for at least a thousand years before the arrival of Europeans. Buried in their kitchen middens, and woven into myths and legends, art, and social and cultural traditions are vivid records of the species they saw and hunted. The raven, eagle, and otter were given roles in creation myths, and marine animal shapes were carved into rattles and helmets and painted onto bowls.

The biological wealth of the Northwest was not lost on the early European explorers either, even though their interest in living resources was primarily commercial. When Captain James Cook explored the Northwest coast in 1778, he immediately established a fur trade with the Native Americans. Although coastal Indians had traded in marine mammal products with inland tribes, the impact on the populations of marine mammals until that time was minimal due to the relative abundance of marine life compared to that of the native populations. But when Captain Cook took his sea otter pelts to the Orient to trade for spices and tea, he began what was to be the near extermination of the sea otter along the entire Northwest coast. Over the next 100 years, white men and Native Americans hunted the sea otter to extinction in this region.

The otter traders were followed by the whalers of Nantucket and New Bedford, who ventured into the Pacific to pursue the great cetaceans that roamed the world's oceans. They supplied an increasing world demand for whale oil, which was used in lamps before the advent of electricity. By 1839, a thriving whaling enterprise was established along the Northwest coast, mostly for sperm and right whales. By the early 1900s, whalers were operating from shore stations, too, further reducing local whale populations, as well as those migrating species that passed near shore.

Sealers—also seeking sources of oil—followed the whalers and obliterated entire populations of pinnipeds on their breeding rookeries. Catch records of whalers and sealers provided an important historical record of species abundance and distribution. They also demonstrated how human predation and activity can alter the survival of a species.

*19th century Tlingit rattles interpreting (left, from top) black oystercatcher, horned puffin, and rhinoceros auklet. Tlingit sea lion helmet (bottom right).*

The impact of human activity was also felt by the great flocks of marine birds that inhabited Puget Sound. In the early 1850s, two army doctors garrisoned on southern Puget Sound compiled a general account of regional animal life. One of them, Lieutenant George Suckley, who had earlier reported California condors along the Columbia River, observed great autumn flocks of sandhill cranes feeding along the Nisqually plains and on "all the prairies near Fort Steilacoom" (Cooper and Suckley, 1859). His comments on how delicious these birds were may account, in part, for the fact that they no longer occur here and are considered a threatened species in Washington State (Washington State Department of Game, 1981).

The surgeon/naturalist described ducks so abundant that Indians used fixed nets to catch great numbers of the birds as they flew along the headlands. A soldier could kill nearly one hundred shorebirds with a single blast of his gun. Today one can only imagine the immensity of those flocks.

While Suckley was prowling the bays near Fort Steilacoom, the pace of settlement along Puget Sound and northward was picking up momentum. By the 1850s, William Bell, C. D. Boren, and Arthur Denny were staking claims on Elliott Bay, and small clusters of families settled at Budd Inlet, Seabeck, Port Ludlow, Penn's Cove, Dungeness, and Bellingham Bay (Denny, 1888). By 1867, a dependable, although seasonal, east-west overland wagon route had been established and immigration to the hospitable bays and beaches of Western Washington began to accelerate.

Newly arrived settlers were primarily preoccupied with survival, however, and there was little time to reflect on natural history. Newspaper accounts from this era report on such practicalities as soil conditions and availability of water. Mammals and birds were usually mentioned only to entice trappers and hunters to the region (Weig, 1880). The settlers may have viewed wildlife as an inexhaustible resource, and probably believed that the huge flocks of ducks and geese could always move on to new habitat as salt marshes were drained, bays dredged and filled, and shorelines developed into busy industrial and commercial waterfronts.

By the first decade of the 20th century, 600,000 people had settled within the 12 counties bordering the Strait of Juan de Fuca, the San Juan Islands, and Puget Sound (Fleming, 1977). In another 60 years the population had nearly quadrupled to 2.2 million, and by the end of the 1980s it is estimated that there will be more than 3 million people within the region.

That the population of greater Puget Sound is more than 250 times larger than at the time of the first census in 1850 is not as extraordinary as the increasing rate at which the region's resources are being consumed. In 1977, nearly 9,000 fishing boats were registered in Washington State and more than 123 million pounds of finfish and 45 million pounds of shellfish were harvested from these waters (Washington Databook, 1977). In the same year, more than 3.5 million people visited the state beaches on Puget Sound.

Marine birds and mammals must continually compete with human enterprise and activity for the available food resources and space. Human development has gradually displaced much of the original wildlife habitat. One example of this loss is described in the *Snohomish Estuary Wetlands Study.* In the late 19th century, the lowlands along the mouth of the Snohomish River consisted of one of the largest salt marsh and tidal flat environments on all of Puget Sound. It hosted enormous flocks of wintering and migrating waterfowl and provided extensive breeding habitat. With the growth of the city of Everett, industrialized development gradually reduced an 11,000-acre wetland habitat to around 2,000 acres (Driscoll, 1979). Gone are the great flocks of waterfowl. Gone, too, are many of the vast nurseries of plant and animal life that sustained them.

Since the late 1960s, increasing attention has been paid to habitat decline, suggesting that perhaps more and more citizens are beginning to sense that they share a common destiny with many of the higher vertebrates. Indeed, that notion was most eloquently expressed by a man whose culture evolved with this region and who understood the relationship of humankind to nature:

If all the beasts were gone
man would die from great loneliness of spirit,
for whatever happens to the beasts
also happens to man.
All things are connected.
Whatever befalls the earth
befalls the sons of the earth.

Chief Sealth—1855

# Habitats and Communities

Puget Sound is a collection of different habitats within which are communities of plants and animals specifically suited to exploit the food and shelter found there. It is the fundamental qualities of these habitats that account for the rich diversity of marine birds and mammals found in the region.

Habitat is the type of environment in which an organism or biological population normally lives and thrives. The term also encompasses environmental requirements for a particular purpose—such as breeding. The breeding habitat of harbor seals, for example, includes the protected shores and islands where seals haul out of the water to give birth and suckle young.

As plants and animals become part of a habitat and begin to exploit its resources, they evolve a workable role in order to survive. The function that an organism (or population of organisms) performs in an environment constitutes a niche. Some animal species are rather cosmopolitan. They can range freely from one habitat to another, fitting their special roles to different ecosystems. The role of the bald eagle and the killer whale, for example, is that of top carnivore, the apex of the food pyramid. Their foraging habits take them over vast areas that comprise many smaller, more specialized habitats. Because killer whales range worldwide, their habitat is all the oceans of the world. All creatures from these giants to primary producers—the plants and phytoplankton—fit into niches of their own and the result is the complex cycle of "eat and be eaten" that makes up the food web.

Sometimes, species not ordinarily expected to have a niche compatible with conditions in Puget Sound may occur here anyway. For example, incursions of oceanic water may bring squid-eating dolphins or rare storm petrels. Migrating whales may wander into inland waters, as though meandering, perhaps seeking food or shelter because of sickness or injury. Some species have found habitats within these waters suitable year-round, and have set up permanent residence. Others are regular seasonal residents here, resting and feeding before moving north or south in annual migrations.

The seasonal variability within these habitats and communities of marine life in the inland sea is almost as diverse as their physical composition. In winter, the open waters of channels and bays are often filled with rafts of loons, grebes, scoters, oldsquaws, and murres. On calm, gray days their innumerable dark bodies stretch out like beads on a table top. Estuaries are frantic with the comings and goings of ducks, geese, and shorebirds. Early in spring the companies of birds reveal individuals pairing off, and by April these legions have headed northward and inland to breed.

The waters and shores of summer are, by comparison, quiet and lonely: the migrants and visitors of winter are gone. There are, however, a few islands, beaches, cliffs and bluffs that are busy with the enterprise of reproduction. Seal pups greet life on a sand spit at Gertrude Island, glaucous-winged gulls squabble over nest sites on Colville Island, and rhinoceros auklets plunge into burrows at Protection Island to feed hungry youngsters. Along Haro Strait, pods of killer whales forage, and minke whales envelop shoals of herring. River otters take their new youngsters on their first fishing forays along Lopez Island. By early fall a cold hand is closing over the far north, and the open reaches of Puget Sound receive the migrant birds moving through the region. Some birds remain through winter; others press further south.

*Pair of adult diving buffleheads*

## Mud and Fine Sand Beaches of Estuaries and Embayments

Beyond the mouths of rivers, where embayments or headlands form protection from sweeping currents and large waves, vast sprawling mudflats form. Fine sediment rich in organic detritus—the food of bottom-dwelling invertebrates and zooplankton—is washed from the interior and from adjoining lowlands. The shallow waters over these sediment flats are often filled with winter populations of common loons, horned grebes, cormorants, and ducks; all come to feed on the zooplankton, fish, crabs, and creatures that live in the mud.

The beaches here are laden with nutritious organic matter that settles out with the ebb and flow of the tides. Snow geese, brant, and whistling swans frequent the intertidal zone along the shores to feed on plant life. The abundant tiny molluscs that filter out the food particles attract tens of thousands of shorebirds to these locations during the fall and winter months. Dunlin, western sandpipers, and plovers ripple over the intertidal area, feeding voraciously along the exposed surface.

In the lower intertidal and shallow subtidal zones, beds of eelgrass grow in the mud and fine sand. The matted root systems of the eelgrass stabilize the fine soil; the blades provide protective cover and feeding locations for a variety of small fish and molluscs, which ultimately become food for the diving birds patrolling above. The herring that spawn in these beds are the essential food of larger fish that in turn sustain many marine mammals, as well as humankind.

At the upper limit of the intertidal zone of mud and fine sand beaches salt marshes may be found. Here, one finds discrete communities of pickleweed, sedge, and bulrush. Surface feeding waterfowl are particularly dependent on this habitat, and in the winter immense congregations of geese and ducks can be found along the marshes of the Nooksack, Skagit, Stillaguamish, and Nisqually Rivers. These marshes are inundated during high tide, which provides a flow of rich organic detritus to the lower mudflats. The regions upland from the marshes are often cultivated and are important feeding and resting areas for wintering waterfowl and shorebirds.

## Coarse Sand and Cobble Beaches

Wave action and constant circulation of waters within the Puget Sound basin, the Strait of Juan de Fuca, and the San Juan Islands have winnowed out the finer sediment from many beaches, leaving coarse sand, gravel, and cobble. Sand beaches are particularly subject to continual movement of sediment particles. They may disappear entirely after a storm, only to reappear within a few months through the process of accretion.

Here the plant and animal life is less diverse. Nevertheless, there are crustaceans, molluscs, and small fish that provide essential food resources for birds. White-winged and surf scoters dive for mussels attached to cobbles. Populations of sharpnose and buffalo sculpins and shiner perch are food for guillemots and grebes. The schooling herring, smelts, sand lances, and sticklebacks are caught by wintering loons, mergansers, murrelets, and rhinoceros auklets.

Along these beaches, turnstones and an occasional black oystercatcher forage. The low tides leave shallow pools where small sole, sculpins, and blennies are stranded. Opportunistic feeders like the great blue heron and yellowlegs wade into these shallows to snap up prey. The steep bluffs backing these beaches—as well as those of finer sediments—are often suitable for excavation by kingfishers and guillemots. A noteworthy example of ideal bluff breeding habitat are the cliffs that tower up from the shores of Protection Island. For centuries, puffins, rhinoceros auklets, and pigeon guillemots have nested and bred in tunnels carved in this glacial till.

*Greater yellowlegs feeding*

# Rocky Shores

*Resting Heermann's gulls*

A characteristic shoreline in northern Puget Sound is rocky cliffs and boulders, mostly of volcanic origin. Exposed to the continuous scouring of current and wave action, these shores offer little surface space to animals and plants unless they are equipped with some mechanism to hold themselves in place. The steepness of slope along these coastal edges determines to some extent the presence and number of species to be found.

Farthest from the water's edge, organisms in the spray zone await the wind-carried salt spray from waves of extreme high tides to provide life-giving moisture. Marine birds, while foraging infrequently here, nevertheless perch on the rocks to rest, clean, and dry out their feathers, and in some cases to nest. In a rocky, pebble-strewn cranny, the female black oystercatcher lays her eggs. Occasionally, on the offshore islands and larger rocks, pelagic cormorants occupy nesting ledges within this zone. Heermann's, glaucous-winged, herring, and western gulls frequently lounge here within easy flying distance to edible morsels washed in by waves. Here, too, come occasional harbor seals, and California and Steller's sea lions to haulout, sun, and sleep.

Although the high tide zone is uncovered most of the time, the intertidal zone is inundated twice a day. Small molluscs and crustaceans are common here, especially limpets, mussels, and crabs, which attract oystercatchers, black turnstones, and an occasional surfbird or wandering tattler.

The lowest tides of the year expose the area of the greatest abundance. At low tide, gulls, shorebirds, and crows descend to dig and poke for food in the exposed mounds of sea grasses and kelp. When this zone is under its protective blanket of water, it is fished regularly by marine birds and mammals. Winter brings flocks of western, red-necked, and horned grebes, which are often joined by red-breasted mergansers, harlequin ducks, and surf scoters.

The subtidal zone is often festooned with bladder kelp that spiral up from holdfasts as thin cords, their fronds radiating over the surface like a canopy. The kelp beds, like the eelgrass, comprise a vegetation system vital to the welfare of marine life. Fish spawn, feed, and seek shelter in the kelp, adjusting their activity to the kelp's sometimes subtle, but often dramatic, movement. Juvenile herring school here in the summer; as adults, they spawn in the kelp in late winter. Sand lances, sculpins, and blennies are also common, while perch, lingcod, and rockfish lurk in the shadows of the deeper water.

Auklets, guillemots, marbled murrelets, and pelagic cormorants are attracted to these fishing spots, patrolling the edges of kelp to surprise their prey. River otters and harbor seals fish here as well. From the surface Bonaparte's gulls and common terns dive for small fish. Herons stand on the mat of kelp to stab at some animal momentarily revealed by a shift in the protective covering.

## Open Waters

## Human-made Habitat

Watching a minke whale cut through a cloud of krill at the entrance to San Juan Channel, or the orcas parade off Roche Harbor, it is easy to grasp the significance of open water to marine life. Nevertheless, there are many vital activities and processes that go largely unnoticed and unappreciated. Phytoplankton, the primary producers in this habitat, provide the dietary base of grazing zooplankton and fish that comprise the diets of the great baleen whales. As waters within entrance channels converge and tidal rips occur, the turbulence stirs nutrients from the bottom, bringing nourishment for copepods and tiny planktonic crustacea swimming near the surface. The copepods are eaten by Cassin's auklets and small fish. The small fish are eaten by larger fish—such as salmon—and by other vertebrates, including rhinoceros auklets, puffins, and murres.

In the open water, scoters, harlequins, goldeneyes, and oldsquaws dive to submerged reefs to feed, sometimes in company with seals and sea lions. Flocks of northern phalaropes and assorted gulls and terns glean their sustenance from the surface.

In the less turbulent open water—in protected bays and on the leeward sides of islands—the great flocks of marine birds come to rest and wait out winter storms. These waters are ideal spots for observing courtship displays in late winter and early spring. Big open water bays—Discovery, Sequim, Skagit, Padilla, and Samish—and inlets like Sinclair often feature displaying red-breasted mergansers, buffleheads, goldeneyes, and white-winged and surf scoters.

The quality of Puget Sound's open waters is still good. As long as it remains so the rich populations of Northwest wildlife will continue to exist here.

The dramatic growth of the Pacific Northwest has occurred at the expense of many coastal wetlands and the quality of its waters. But though some wildlife populations dwindle as people increase in numbers, other species thrive and find ways to exploit what humans create.

Dock pilings, jetties, and marinas that initially disrupt established wildlife, eventually attract pioneering marine species. Protozoa, sea anemones, and sponges are quick to exploit newly opened niches. Flatworms and polychaete annelids are found in these locations, too, but it's the molluscs and fish that establish themselves here that attract the marine birds. The most common crustaceans found around waterfront structures are copepods, amphipods, isopods, and shrimps. They are consumed by diving and dabbling ducks. The surf and white-winged scoters dive for edible mussels attached to pilings along ferry slips, and occasionally red-breasted mergansers, horned grebes, and cormorants feed on small perch, sculpins, and sole.

Some waterfront structures are used by birds as lookouts for prey and as places to build nests. Where abandoned docks provide an overlook, wintering merlins and resident kingfishers scan beaches and waters. In more isolated areas, peregrine falcons sometimes use these conditions to good advantage. Cormorants "dry out" wet wings and preen while perched on docks and pilings. At Dungeness and Port Angeles, pelagic cormorants have established small colonies using pilings to support their nests.

Even dredge spoils are sometimes exploited by marine birds. Such deposits along the eastern edge of March Point have become important nesting areas for glaucous-winged gulls. A dredge spoil island off Everett supports a colony of arctic terns.

*A murre maneuvering in pursuit of prey*

# Forces that Affect Marine Birds and Mammals

## Habitat Modification

There are external threats to the survival of every living creature. Animals are hunted by other animals. They starve when there is a lack of food, or they are unable to compete for it. They die as a result of disease, parasites, and exposure due to severe weather. They suffer reproduction failures when there is a lack of suitable breeding habitat. These adversities may foster the rise of one population of animals while causing the demise of another. In this delicate and ever-changing balancing act, man is the one species that can cause greater changes in less time than nature itself. Thus, human beings must exercise considerable care if they are to control their impacts upon natural habitats and wildlife populations.

In the 1970s, state and federal laws were enacted to protect the marine habitat. Federal Executive Orders 11990 and 11988 and the Washington Shoreline Management Act extend protection to marine wildlife and consider the destruction or excessive alteration of wetlands contrary to the public interest. Policy, however, is one thing; practice is another. The diversity and size of marine wildlife populations continue to decline despite policies designed to protect them.

*Young elephant seal*

As human population expanded exponentially worldwide, natural habitats suitable for sustaining a diversity of marine plants and animals gave way to the need for rich agricultural ground, commercially navigable waterways, and waterfront land for ports, industry, and recreation. Modification and destruction of the earth's natural environments continues. One startling result of extensive environmental degradation is that an estimated 20 percent of animal species currently existing may become extinct by the year 2000 (Barney, 1980). This rate of demise of species is unprecedented.

The term "habitat loss," however, really means that when one type of habitat diminishes, another gains. The total amount of space available for habitat is constant; the earth neither gains nor loses total available space. Both nature and humans, however, rearrange and modify this space in ways that may benefit some species while adversely affecting others.

Over the last 100 years, shorelines and major river deltas of Washington have been significantly modified by human activity. More than half of the Skagit River Delta wetland wildlife habitat has been converted to agricultural plains and industrial landfill. On the Snohomish River Delta—second only to the Skagit in flood plain area and annual discharge—less than one quarter (10 sq. km) of the original wetlands area still exists (Bortleson et al., 1980). The Stillaguamish, Lummi, and Samish Deltas have undergone significant changes. Through diking, industrialization has all but eliminated the wetlands along the mouths of the Duwamish and Puyallup Rivers. Of the larger river estuaries in Puget Sound, only the Nisqually, Nooksack, Dungeness, and Skokomish still retain much of their original wetlands habitat. Of the smaller systems, only those emptying into Hood Canal—the Dosewalips, Quilcene, Duckabush, and Hamma Hamma Rivers—remain relatively pristine.

The most obvious and common ways to alter wetlands are physical changes. Low marine borderlands have been significantly altered by building dikes, channelling rivers, and draining and filling marshes and wetlands. Initially, these patterns drown and smother existing vegetation. Over time, water temperature and salinity levels change as salt water is excluded and fresh water allowed to intrude. These two variables directly affect the types of flora and fauna that live in marshy areas and therefore ultimately upset the balance of the food web, and destroy camouflage for nests and protective cover from predators.

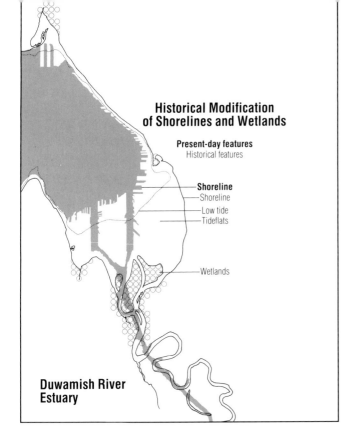

### Historical Modification
### of Shorelines and Wetlands

**Present-day features**
Historical features

**Shoreline**
Shoreline
Low tide
Tideflats

Wetlands

**Duwamish River
Estuary**

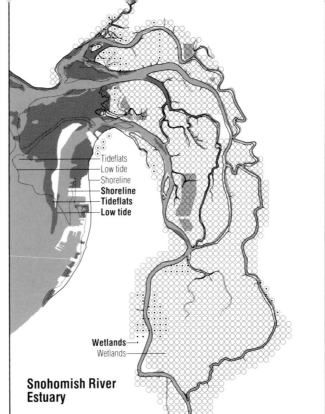

Tideflats
Low tide
Shoreline
**Shoreline**
**Tideflats**
**Low tide**

**Wetlands**
Wetlands

**Snohomish River
Estuary**

In some areas dredging of marine waters is necessary to maintain navigable waterways, to provide small boat moorage, and to improve and expand port facilities. But this activity also profoundly affects marine wildlife habitat by disrupting the benthic life and suspending sediments in the water column. Suspended and exposed unoxidized sediments create a high biological oxygen demand, which can destroy plants and animals. Dredging also exposes toxic materials that may have accumulated in the substrate. As these toxins are released, they contaminate the water column and slowly infiltrate the food chain.

When dredging is done in shallow embayments, marine plants such as eelgrass are ripped up. The destruction of eelgrass beds further reduces the food available to those ducks, geese, and swans favoring this plant and to those birds and mammals that feed on the fish inhabiting these retreats. A final indignity of dredging is that sometimes the spoils are dumped in other marine areas, smothering the bottom life. This problem may be mitigated, however, when habitats are created by dredge spoils, as was Jetty Island near Everett.

Structures built along the shoreline and into the water have both short- and long-term effects on the marine environment. Initially, structures built into the water modify local flow patterns, which ultimately change conditions necessary to sustain established plant and animal communities. Marinas—which are actually artificial harbors—can alter water circulation and exposure to wave energy. Thus, within the moorage basin the dissolved oxygen level of the water will be lowered and pollutants will be concentrated. Hydrocarbons, and metals from anti-

fouling paints and electrodes on small craft will gradually build up in fish and shellfish and eventually enter the diets of foraging marine birds and mammals.

Construction of piers, docks, pilings, and bulkheads temporarily disrupts the substrate, increases the turbidity of an area's waters, and displaces its animals. Bulkheads constructed along the shore or in a wetland eliminate that land for use by resident marine animals.

Log booms, although temporary structures, can preclude access of marine birds to food supplies. These booms float over shallow subtidal, intertidal, and marsh areas at high tide and settle on the substrate at low tide. As the booms alternately compress and shadow the sea bed, they alter the benthic algae. Bark from the logs also settles onto the substrate, altering its composition as well. After the rafts are removed, several months are required for plants and animals to recolonize an area (Driscoll, 1979).

Finally, it is important to note that not all habitats critical to marine birds and mammals are found in the narrow coastal zone. Many marine birds depend on feeding, resting, and nesting areas inland or far removed from Puget Sound. Interference to these remote habitats can be as devastating to the birds as the dredging of a shallow mud bay. Nor should one forget the importance of freshwater spawning grounds to salmonids or of the distant breeding grounds of whales and pinnipeds. The cumulative effect of logging practices that increase stream siltation, alter flood patterns, and raise water temperatures may be as insidious as a major vacation home development on a critical nesting area.

# Pollution

In the past, Puget Sound was often a convenient and economical depository for undesirable wastes. Raw sewage, waste fish products, and wood wastes were dumped directly into these waters. As the area's population grew and its industrial base expanded, the amount and diversity of municipal and industrial wastes increased.

At the same time, streets, highways, and parking lots were paved, causing more rapid runoff of rainfall. In its natural state, soil provides temporary storage, filtration, and bacterial action of ground waters; but paved surfaces carry contaminants more rapidly into marine waters. These contaminants accumulate in groundwater and river systems, through which they travel great distances to debilitate sensitive regions far from the source of contamination. In Western Washington, the termini of this extensive system are the rich deltas and estuaries of Puget Sound.

Today, industrial discharges—although they have been reduced over the past decade—still contain burdens of pesticides, phenols, metals, and polychlorinated biphenyls. Runoff from urban areas frequently contains oil, grease, heavy metals, and coliform bacteria. In rural areas runoffs contain pesticides and fertilizers from agriculture, leachates from log-staging areas, heavy metals from the atmosphere and natural sources, and coliform bacteria.

Many of these toxicants are attracted to the small mineral and organic particles suspended in the water column in Puget Sound. Because they are adsorbed onto the surface of these particles, toxicants dissolved in water are usually slight, but concentrations on suspended particulate matter and in the seabed sediments—which are formed by these settled particles—are high. Similarly, in the biota, toxicants are more concentrated in the life forms that extract their food from organic matter in the sediments or filter it from suspended matter.

Accidental spills and industrial dumping practices have led to very high levels of toxic materials in the sediments of harbors near urban centers. In Puget Sound, the most severely polluted sediments are in areas where large quantities of industrial waste products were once dumped on unused tideflats or in deep bays. Although these practices have ceased, the contaminants remain. Commencement Bay is a case in point.

Not enough is known of the long-term biological effects of the toxic materials in the environment. What is known is that many are slow acting, long lived, and persistent. As they move through the food chain, from primary producer to prey to predator, they become more and more concentrated.

Significant quantities of toxic chemicals have already made their way into the bodies of marine animals and they have been correlated with liver lesions in fish and assorted biological abnormalities in invertebrates (Malins et al., 1980). Bottom-dwelling creatures such as crabs, clams, and worms in Budd Inlet, Sinclair Inlet, Commencement Bay, and Elliott Bay exhibit the highest levels of contaminants. Because these creatures are important to the diets of many marine birds and mammals, they too are affected. Indeed, birth defects observed in harbor seal pups in southern Puget Sound appear to be related to high levels of chemical pollutants in the pups' tissues.

Although pesticides and toxicants build up slowly and can result in gradual degradation of the environment and its inhabitants, there are other dangers which can occur swiftly, without warning, and with devastating effect. Accidental spills of hazardous materials pose such a danger. Between 1974 and 1979, the U.S. Coast Guard recorded more than 2,500 individual spills of oil and other hazardous materials in the Strait of Juan de Fuca and greater Puget Sound (Fulton, 1981). These spills resulted in nearly a quarter of a million gallons of contaminants entering the region's waters. Only slightly more than 20 percent of this volume was ever recovered.

Most of these spills were minor and appear to have had little impact on marine animals. Some of them, however, represent the kind of threat this type of accident poses to marine life. An example is a 100,000-gallon spill of hydrochloric acid in Commencement Bay in 1976. Had such a spill occurred earlier in the year when concentrations of wintering birds roost on the water, it would have been disastrous.

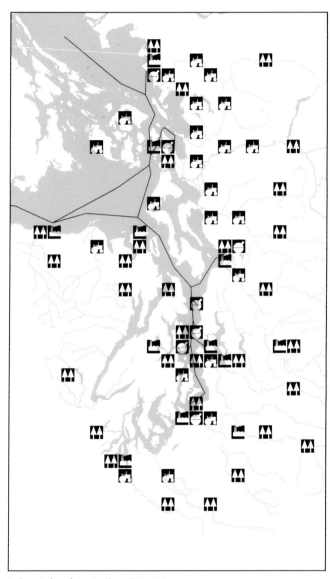

Industrial and Agricultural Activity

   Agriculture
   Oil and Chemicals Production
   Forest Products Production
   Heavy Industry
   Oil and Chemicals
   Waterborne Transportation Routes

The present tanker route for oil transport and a proposed underwater pipeline across northern Puget Sound pose further threat of accidental spills to marine birds and mammals and to their environment. If a spill occurred in these waters, crude oil could move within days to the shores of Padilla Bay, Whidbey Island, the San Juans, and the tideflats of Port Susan and Skagit Bays (Cox et al., 1980). In a critical time of year, an oil spill could devastate entire populations of waterfowl. Ducks, geese, swans, and shorebirds might find a large portion of their food base contaminated or suffer the more immediate threats of oiling.

The consequences of oiling to marine birds and mammals are varied but usually deadly. If they ingest oil by eating contaminated food or by cleaning it off their feathers or fur, they can sicken and die. Birds are likely to become chilled and develop pneumonia because feathers matted with oil lose their insulating capability. Oiled feathers can also result in a loss of buoyancy, causing birds that rest and feed in the water to drown. Contamination of eggs can cause hatching failures, and ingestion of oil by nestlings can cause growth abnormalities in essential organs (Manuwal et al., 1981).

The degree of risk to bird populations from oiling is related to the way birds depend upon the marine environment and the susceptibility of these environments to oil spills. Birds that roost on the water at night can be trapped by floating slicks. Birds that dive to feed or avoid predators can become coated as they enter the water and surface through the film. Both birds and mammals can suffer from the long-term loss of food resources. It should also be noted that some species have a very significant percentage of their entire west coast population using Puget Sound waters (brant, snow geese, rhinoceros auklets), and exposure to oiling affects entire populations, not just individual birds.

Although the overall variety of species of plants and animals will reestablish itself over a relatively short period, one study of a spill area showed that even after 15 months, abundance and density of individual species was only half that of original population sizes (Vanderhorst et al., 1980). It is these populations that form interdependent links in the complex food webs upon which so many marine birds and mammals depend.

# People Pressure—
# Recreation and Vessel Traffic

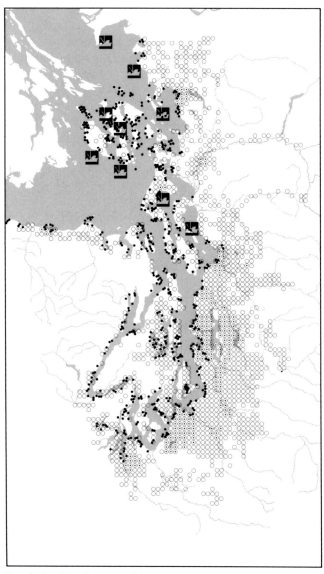

Population Distribution and Marine Recreation Areas

- Over 500 people
- Urban Areas
- Marinas, Boating Anchorages, Marine Parks
- Commercial Fishing Areas

People affect the environment directly by modifying or polluting it, but they also affect it indirectly. People of the Pacific Northwest enjoy the marine areas as boaters, beachwalkers, and nature observers. As the area's population grows and people demand greater access to public waterways, beaches, marshlands, and marine parks, unintentional habitat interference becomes a serious threat to marine animals.

With more boat owners, out-of-the-way rocks, islands, and quiet bays will become more and more accessible. Many of these areas have been set aside as preserves to protect wildlife. In these areas even the most benign human activity may unwittingly interfere with nesting, feeding, and resting of marine birds and mammals.

Public marinas and boating rendezvous number nearly 300 along greater Puget Sound and the Strait of Juan de Fuca (Washington Marine Atlas, 1974). These facilities give the boating public an opportunity to explore otherwise inaccessible waters and shores. Marine bird breeding colonies on offshore rocks and islands and harbor seal pupping beaches are no longer isolated from human traffic. Unfortunately, the most intensive recreational activity occurs during the late spring and summer— the same time that marine animals require isolation to breed successfully.

When a curious boater takes to shore to wander or walk a pet, the effects often can be disastrous. A pet left to run through a marine bird colony during breeding or nesting season can create havoc. As cormorants plunge from the bluffs, or ground-nesting, glaucous-winged gulls swirl into the air, they leave their eggs or young exposed to the elements and predators. In the hysteria, eggs are broken, and young birds trampled or tumbled from nests.

Even a person casually walking along a beach can be disruptive. Low tide—a time that often attracts inquisitive vacationers, beachcombers, and clam diggers—is also the time when many prey species are exposed. When human traffic along these locations is intense, feeding birds cannot reach their food sources.

Recreational boaters can penetrate feeding waters in shallow draft boats, frightening birds from their foraging. In the open water off shore, commercial ships and recreational boats may interrupt birds and mammals feeding in entrance channels and tidal rips. These waters are heavily travelled by many commercial vessels—passenger ferries, barges, freighters, tankers, and fishing boats. To some degree it appears that birds feeding on the water have learned to avoid the 1,000-ft-wide vessel traffic lanes.

Some marine birds and mammals are affected by fishing and other vessel activities in these waters. Each year, harbor and dall porpoises, seals, and sea lions become entangled in gillnets. Guillemots, auklets, murres, and occasionally puffins and loons are also snagged and drowned in fishing nets.

There are no easy answers to the question of how to balance the scale between the needs of marine wildlife and those of people. Each time a question arises, a new set of circumstances must be weighed and judged. In this book as each family or species of birds and mammals is discussed, we will try to portray how they may be particularly sensitive to changes in their habitat caused by human activity.

*Rhinoceros auklet flapping wings*
*off Protection Island*

*Gulls and alcids feeding on
herring in a tidal rip*

# Marine Birds

What distinguishes a marine bird from any other bird? Such a bird spends all or a good portion of its life in association with the sea. It utilizes the food, shelter, resting, and breeding locations that are part of the marine system. Its presence may be periodic or continuous; indeed, a survey of marine species of Puget Sound indicates that many of them spend at least a portion of their lives elsewhere. Loons, grebes, geese, and shorebirds pass through the region while migrating, or they winter here then return to freshwater lakes and shores of the interior or far north to breed. Some cormorants and gulls, on the other hand, remain here throughout the year, although they may wander widely. Rhinoceros auklets and tufted puffins are found here from early spring into fall, at which time most of them move to the open coast and offshore waters.

Waterfowl and shorebirds share physical adaptations suitable for exploiting the resources of Puget Sound. Among the families of birds there exists a remarkable range of specialized beaks, feet, and body sizes for gaining access to food and breeding habitat. A snow goose, for example, possesses a thick blunt bill with serrated margins and a tongue edged with sharp denticles. Such equipment is just right for holding and tearing out eelgrass blades and bullrush shoots. A rhinoceros auklet snaps up fish with a heavy, bony bill and holds them with its partially cornified tongue while it continues to catch other fish. The Cassin's auklet's bill is more spoonlike. It can carry a large "package" of food back to its nestling by combining it with the food stored in its throat pouch. Probing birds, which feed along mudflats and beaches of fine sediment, show still another form of specialized bill. Long-billed dowitchers wade the shallows or salt marshes poking a four-inch bill into the mud to "feel" for animals hidden there. A black oystercatcher, prowling over the raw rocky coastline can pry limpets off rocks and pummel crabs with its long stout beak.

A webbed foot is an asset to any aquatic bird and is part of the equipment of most of the marine species. Cormorants possess a relatively large webbed area; all four of their toes are connected with webbing, unlike swans, geese and ducks that have only three of their toes webbed. Diving ducks have slightly longer toes and a larger webbed area than their comparably sized relatives that dabble in shallow water and walk along the shore. These walking waterfowl have legs positioned farther forward than the divers and amble along on well-padded feet. Grebes, coots, and phalaropes swim with the assistance of the lobate extensions along their toes rather than webs in between. Puffins and auklets have webbing but also have strong, sharp, curved "nails" on the tips of their toes that, along with their bills are used to excavate nesting burrows.

Shorebirds are both long and short legged. The quick dashes of sanderlings to and from the water line are accomplished on toothpick-like legs that move as blurs beneath their compact bodies. The yellowlegs is, in contrast, a stately wader, with long tarsi that keep the bird aloft as it searches for small fish in shallow bays.

There are subtle differences among marine birds in body and wing shape as well. Diving loons, western grebes, and cormorants have long serpentine necks and tapered bodies. Ideal forms, indeed, for threading over and through the offshore beds of eelgrass or kelp pursuing prey. Guillemots, auklets, murres, and other alcids have dense, heavy bodies relative to their size. Their weight helps them dive to feeding depth rapidly and maintain direction in tricky currents. These same species, which might be considered the Northern Hemisphere's penguins, have very sleek and narrow wings set far back on their bodies, which they use like paddles to propel themselves.

Some important generalist species are also tied to the marine environment. The nesting density of bald eagles in northern Puget Sound is higher than anywhere in the United States except Alaska. An efficient predator and scavenger, the eagle forages waters and beaches for living prey and whatever carrion the evening's high tide deposits. Large gulls and the northwest race of the common crow share a lifestyle similar to that of the eagle. These birds occasionally catch live marine animals and feed on the continuous spread of edible refuse washed up on the beaches.

For a few marine birds—such as the brant, snow goose, peregrine falcon, and rhinoceros auklet—the Puget Sound region is especially important. A significant portion of the birds' west coast populations reside here at some time during the year. To lose access to resources would be disastrous to these populations. Other species here represent the essential diversity and web of interdependence that holds the system together.

# Loons
## *Gaviidae*

There is a moment in April when winter releases the last of her grip on Puget Sound, giving way to the warm and scented breath of spring. Along Padilla Bay the brant felt it as surely as I did. They moved in restless, irregular lines, flying above an incessant clamor of mixed voices assembled on the waters below. Canvasbacks, scoters, buffleheads, and scaup were all touched by the first faint urges to depart northward to nesting grounds.

Amid the assorted shapes and colors, I saw a single bird, distinguished from the rest by manner and profile. Its form had been honed to efficiency by evolution and the silhouetted lines spoke to the diving and fishing life of the bird. It was a yellow-billed loon, its colors already changing from drab winter gray, sitting flat on the water. The wings of the yellow-billed loon are set far back on its body and it appears to have no tail at all in contrast to the stiletto-like bill jutting out from its thick head and neck. When partially submerged it is able, like others of this family, to reduce buoyancy by compressing its feathers and expelling much of the trapped air. Watching this streamlined bird from a distance it was difficult to appreciate the size of this large loon. I knew, however, that its open foot could easily cover the top of my fist, and that some of these solid-boned birds weigh up to 14 pounds.

Of the four loons wintering in Puget Sound the yellow-billed is the most rare. Like the red-throated and arctic loons, these birds restrict their breeding to the far north, nesting near the Arctic Circle. Only the common loons breed as far south as the northern contiguous states.

The different species of loons tend to choose separate foraging habitats. The red-throated and yellow-billed loons exploit shallow waters over reefs and near shore. Common loons normally feed slightly farther out from shore. Arctic loons, although occasionally sharing feeding waters with common loons, prefer deep channels and offshore reefs.

Loons can dive deep to feed. Common loons plunge as deep as 60 meters, where they may remain to forage for a minute or more. They also dive to flee from predators such as bald eagles. At times pairs of eagles will team up to pursue an arctic loon to exhaustion. Each time the bird surfaces one of the eagles forces the loon to dive until, unable to dive again, the winded bird is plucked from the surface.

The loon's versatility on and under the water does not, however, help these birds get into the air. Because their legs are set far back on their body, loons have to make a long, foot-slapping run in order to become airborne. The exception is the red-throated loon, which can take off more directly from the water. Once in the air, however, the flight is swift and direct. Indeed, at top speed the flight of the common loon has been clocked at well over 60 miles per hour.

Both sexes of loons are similar in color, patterning, and size. All four species assume the gray-above, white-below winter plumage. The species are somewhat distinct in their size differences with the smallest, the red-throated, only a third the body weight of the largest, the common and yellow-billed loons. The arctic loon is only slightly larger than the red-throated.

Arctic and red-throated loons are particularly vulnerable to oiling because they form large feeding flocks that dive together, and they roost on open water. Because they are inclined to feed in remote waters, loons are not generally bothered by intense boating activity and beach visitors that disturb birds feeding closer to shore.

*Arctic loon in winter plumage*

## Common Loon
### *Gavia immer*

Length 61 cm (24 in)
Wingspread to 149 cm (58 in)

**Status and Distribution** Arriving as early as September and staying into May, these birds are common winter residents and migrants as well as uncommon summer visitors to the region. Singly and in pairs, common loons begin to gather in Hood Canal and Puget Sound by late fall. The population reaches its greatest density here by spring.

**Food and Critical Habitat** Common loons favor small and medium-sized fish—flounders, herring, sculpins, and shiner perch—as well as amphipods, crabs, and shrimps. They forage in both nearshore and open-water habitats, where they sometimes dive over reefs. They are particularly fond of fishing the edges of estuarine waters, though they prefer to rest on open water.

*Diving common loon in breeding plumage.*

## Arctic Loon
*Gavia arctica*

Length 46 cm (18 in)
Wingspread 120 cm (47 in)

**Status and Distribution** Arctic loons are common winter residents in the Strait of Juan de Fuca and Puget Sound. These birds are the members of the loon family most likely to form sizeable flocks. From October into May their fishing groups sometimes number in the hundreds.

Significant feeding areas for arctic loons include Speiden and Guemes Channels, and Wasp and Obstruction Passages out to Peavine Passage. The west side of Cypress Island hosts large numbers of these loons, particularly along Strawberry Bay. They also frequent the waters off Deer Harbor, Harvey Channel, the southern end of San Juan Channel, and Deception Pass.

**Food and Critical Habitat** Arctic loons feed on small fish—such as shiner perch and herring—when in Puget Sound. They follow the schooling fish in open water, well off shore, and may dive for over a minute when pursuing a meal. Feeding and gathering areas in Puget Sound important to arctic loons are generally those passages with strong tidal rips.

## Red-throated Loon
*Gavia stellata*

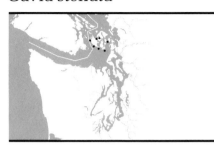

Length 43 cm (17 in)
Wingspread 112 cm (44 in)

**Status and Distribution** Common winter residents throughout Puget Sound, these birds occasionally remain through the summer as nonbreeding birds.

Red-throated loons are found over the entire Puget Sound region, but in recent years they have been well represented, especially throughout the fall and winter (October into May), in the waters surrounding San Juan Island, along Cypress Island at Strawberry Bay, and near Deer Harbor on Orcas Island.

**Food and Critical Habitat** The smallest of the loons, red-throated loons are capable of diving to ten meters or more in pursuit of sand lances and other bottomfish. They also consume molluscs and crustaceans. Red-throated loons commonly feed in bays and inlets; preferring shallow nearshore waters, particularly those over mudflats and associated estuaries.

## Yellow-billed Loon
*Gavia adamsii*

Length 63 cm (25 in)
Wingspread 152 cm (59 in)

**Status and Distribution** Rare winter residents on Puget Sound, a few yellow-billed loons are seen each winter in the northern Sound from Point Roberts to Bellingham Bay. Occasionally, they can be found feeding near Port Angeles, in Padilla Bay, Hood Canal, and Eld Inlet in southern Puget Sound during the winter months.

**Food and Critical Habitat** These large loons have a diet composed of fish—sculpins, rockfish, tomcod, and crustaceans—shrimps, and small crabs. A yellow-billed loon observed at Padilla Bay was consuming small crabs retrieved from the eelgrass beds. Like the common loons, these birds prefer inshore waters of bays and inlets.

*Red-throated loons—
male (left) in breeding plumage,
female in winter garb*

# Grebes
## *Podicipedidae*

Unlike the algae laden waters of summer, spring waters in the San Juan Islands are particularly clear. As our ferry drifted gently to the slip at Orcas Island I could follow the angled rays of sunlight and peer into the depths. Off to one side, near pilings coated with marine life, horned grebes were plying the currents for food. They bobbed about on the transparent tension of the surface, not particularly concerned about the ponderous boat pressing in against the shore. The pair, already in spring plumage, made graceful dives, curving down through the surface, and then—legs pumping furiously—descending in a corkscrew path into deeper water. I judged that the wash and swirl of the ferry had stirred food from the bottom and the birds were there to search it out.

As we departed the grebes were still fishing comfortably in this niche, unchallenged by other marine birds. One of the birds popped to the surface with a tiny sculpin's tail protruding out from the edge of its beak. Then, with a shake of the bird's head, its catch disappeared.

Substantial numbers of grebes come to Puget Sound in late summer and fall and stay through the winter. The Sound is an important wintering area for large numbers of western, red-necked, and horned grebes. Eared grebes are less common, and the pied-billed grebe is rare indeed on Sound waters. In the spring, breeding birds head northeast, retiring to the freshwater lakes and ponds of the Canadian interior to raise their broods.

The name Podiceps means "rump-footed," and refers to the placement of the bird's legs, which are far to the rear of its body. This anatomical arrangement enhances the bird's ability to dive and maneuver underwater, but renders it notoriously helpless on land.

Rather than being web-footed like most water birds on the Sound, these species have evolved—like coots and phalaropes—fleshy lobes along the edges of each toe. This lobate webbing gives grebes the ability to propel themselves with ease on and beneath the water, allowing them to compete effectively for food resources.

The size differences between species to some degree broadens the range of prey they take and reduces interspecific competition for the same food. The small horned grebes fish shallow inshore waters, consuming a variety of tiny fish and crustaceans like mysids and shrimps. Red-necked and western grebes prefer diving for herring, sticklebacks, and smelts in open water.

Like loons, the red-necked, horned, and eared grebes molt their colorful spring and summer feathers and acquire a somber gray winter plumage over head, back, and wings. However, the western grebe maintains essentially the same plumage throughout the year. In all grebes feather color and patterning is identical in the male and female. Their plumages are counter-shaded and the light undercoloring, when seen in the water from below, reduces the starkness of their silhouettes against the lighted surface.

The coloring pattern is an effective camouflage for this fishing bird. Grebes, like loons, float along the surface dipping their heads beneath the surface as they swim, "scouting" like a skin diver who snorkels along the surface looking for fish or promising locations before diving. A well-defined silhouette sitting on the surface is likely to frighten fish away.

Because grebes maintain their flocks when feeding and roosting, and dive in the presence of danger, members of this family of marine birds are among the most vulnerable to oiling. A spill would likely contaminate many birds at a time. Western grebes, which form large winter flocks on the Sound, are particularly vulnerable. They flock where oil tanker and boat traffic is intense, such as in Fidalgo Bay off March Point, near Bellingham, and in Quartermaster Harbor in southern Puget Sound.

# Red-necked Grebe
*Podiceps grisegena*

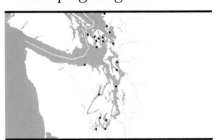

Length 33 cm (13 in)
Wingspread 81 cm (32 in)

**Status and Distribution**     A common migrant and winter resident from September into May throughout Puget Sound, the red-necked grebe is seen singly or in small groups feeding in offshore waters. Early in the 20th century thousands of this species were reported gathered near Port Townsend (Dawson, 1909). Reports of flocking red-necked grebes in the late 1970s suggest only hundreds of birds now gather prior to migrating out of northern Puget Sound in the spring (Gardner, 1979).

Although they are fairly common throughout the Sound, these birds favor Padilla Bay, Hale Pass, Drayton Harbor, and the southern end of San Juan Channel. They fish in Thatcher, Wasp, Obstruction, and Peavine Passes, as well as Harney and Speiden Channels. In southern Puget Sound, Budd, Case, and Carr Inlets are important feeding locations for red-necked grebes.

**Food and Critical Habitat**     Offshore and nearshore waters provide wintering habitat for these grebes. They dive for sticklebacks, herring, and sculpins in estuaries and in entrance channels. Crustaceans may also be important to their diets.

# Horned Grebe
*Podiceps auritus*

Length 24 cm (9 in)
Wingspread 62 cm (24 in)

**Status and Distribution**     Common winter residents throughout Puget Sound, horned grebes can be found from September until May, at which time they depart for their breeding grounds in southeastern Washington. Some nonbreeding birds remain in Puget Sound throughout the summer.

**Food and Critical Habitat**     Horned grebes feed in open waters, major channels, sheltered bays, and estuaries. The birds patrol singly, in pairs, or in small groups, diving for sculpins, sticklebacks, shiner perch, and a variety of crustaceans that includes amphipods and shrimps.

These little grebes also forage in human-altered habitats, such as marinas and busy harbors. During the winter they frequently gather, for example, at the seaward end of the locks at Shilshole Bay and along the edges of Elliott Bay. The effects on the birds of exposure to contaminants in the environment is unknown. In less developed locations, Admiralty Inlet is a particularly important feeding area for this marine bird, at times supporting hundreds of them.

*Horned grebe in winter plumage*

# Eared Grebe
*Podiceps nigricollis*

Length 23 cm (9 in)
Wingspread 59 cm (23 in)

**Status and Distribution**    The eared grebe is the smallest of the grebes found in the Pacific Northwest. It is an uncommon migrant and winter resident from September to May in Puget Sound. This species undoubtedly is sometimes confused with the horned grebe because of its similar winter plumage. Although uncommon, these grebes are seen with some frequency. They have been sighted in Penn Cove, Padilla Bay, and protected bays along the Strait of Juan de Fuca (Gardner, 1979). The ferry slip at Anacortes is a popular feeding site.

**Food and Critical Habitat**    Eating shrimps, mysids, amphipods, and occasionally fish, these birds feed farther from shore than the horned grebes. They forage in channels, over reefs, and over tidal flats inside estuarine waters.

*Diving eared grebes in breeding plumage*

*"Dueling" western grebes*

## Western Grebe
*Aechmophorus occidentalis*

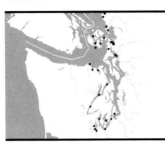

Length 46 cm (18 in)
Wingspread 102 cm (40 in)

**Status and Distribution**  The western is the largest of the grebes found in Washington State. It is a common winter resident on Puget Sound. Some nonbreeding birds remain here throughout the summer, but most of the local population begins to concentrate in late September and early October, remaining only through April.

Waters of northeast Samish and Bellingham Bays are extremely important to this species; between 10,000 and 20,000 birds have been estimated to gather here during winter. Fidalgo and Padilla Bays and the waters of Guemes Channel out to Hat Island host up to 5,000 birds. Skagit, Dungeness, Sequim, and Discovery Bays are also important. Waters off Fidalgo Bay from Crandal Spit around to March Point are important for surf smelt and Pacific herring. Western grebes are quick to exploit this food resource. Other areas in nothern Puget Sound used by this species are Deception Pass, Portage Bay, Hales Passage, Lummi Bay, Drayton Harbor, and Birch Bay.

In the southern Sound, Case, Carr, Eld, Henderson, and Budd Inlets are important wintering waters, along with Quartermaster Harbor, The Narrows, and the Nisqually Flats (Gardner, 1979). Hood Canal is also fished by western grebes.

**Food and Critical Habitat**  The scientific name of this bird means "spearbearing." It is an appropriate name, for this grebe uses its bill to stab and snap up its prey. Western grebes consume Pacific herring, sculpins, shiner perch, and smelts, and sometimes small crabs and shrimps.

As a rule, these birds prefer deep offshore waters but will often move closer to shore in bays, harbors, mudflats, and estuaries when fishing there is good. Off March Point near Anacortes, scattered flocks totaling thousands of birds feed at the edges of oil tanker, fishing, and pleasure boat lanes. Large numbers of wintering western grebes concentrate also in waters near Bremerton's Sinclair Inlet in the shadows of the battleships anchored there.

## Pied-billed Grebe
*Podilymbus podiceps*

Length 23 cm (9 in)
Wingspread 59 cm (23 in)

**Status and Distribution**  This species rarely visits Puget Sound during the winter as it prefers fresh water year round. In severe winters, however, when interior lakes, ponds, and river sloughs are frozen, the pied-bills move into the Sound for sustenance. They tend to maintain small groups through the winter, often appearing in groups of four to six birds.

**Food and Critical Habitat**  These stocky birds follow rivers to the estuaries where they seek shrimps and small fish, such as sculpins and sticklebacks.

# Albatrosses
## *Diomedeidae*

My first trip in Washington's coastal waters was when I was a young man working on a fishing boat. We left Neah Bay in pre-dawn darkness, and arrived at the entrance to the Strait of Juan de Fuca wrapped in a shroud of fog. We cruised slowly, intent on finding a school of salmon bunching up for a dash to the waters of the interior. Then, as now, my first interest was birds, and while the other crew members watched nervously for signs of fish I was content to follow the flights and dives of the tufted puffins, murres, and Cassin's auklets in the waters around us.

By midmorning the fog had cleared and swells began to build, dropping our craft into troughs so deep we lost sight of the horizon. On one such plunge I caught sight of a long narrow-winged glider heading toward us up the tunnel of the wave trough. It was much larger than the few gulls that had followed us out to this distance. It did not move its wings at all, but rather rode a cushion of air over the water. It would descend to within a few feet of the surface only to rise again, then turn and wheel with just the slightest tilt of its wings.

The bird I saw was a black-footed albatross. This species—like others of its family—wanders with the wind. Indeed, with its goose-sized body, in order to become airborne and remain there to forage the albatross depends on the presence of steady, moderate to high winds. Black-footed albatrosses are among the most pelagic of all marine birds. They return to land to breed on the northwestern chain of the Hawaiian Islands for only a few months out of the year. These birds do not breed until they are at least five-years old, and a male and female generally pair for life.

## Black-footed Albatross
### *Diomedea nigripes*

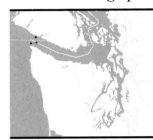

Length 71 cm (28 in)
Wingspread 205 cm (80 in)

**Status and Distribution**  This species occurs commonly from April through October well off shore along the Washington coast. It rarely wanders into Puget Sound, and both early and recent records find the bird no farther east than the entrance to the Strait of Juan de Fuca.

**Food and Critical Habitat**  A pelagic scavenger, the black-footed albatross searches the ocean's surface for edible refuse, including the discards of ships' galleys or scraps from fishing boats. Its primary foods are squids, crabs, and surface fish taken in open waters of the North Pacific where low-temperature, nutrient-rich waters sustain high biological productivity.

# Shearwaters and Fulmars
## *Procellariidae*

Perhaps among the greatest of travelling birds, shearwaters are not as familiar to humans as are the gulls and albatrosses for they are not inclined to follow ships. Their rapid and confident flight distinguishes them from the gulls, however. They cut in fast and low on layers of an air cushion above the water, sometimes nicking the crest of a swell as they turn to slide down its back. Their name, shearwater, is indicative of the impression they make on the observer as they continuously slice in over the waters.

Both light and dark phases of the fulmar occur in the North Pacific. Of the two, the dark gray phase is more often seen within the Strait of Juan de Fuca. Also birds of the offshore waters, fulmars, unlike shearwaters, will follow boats and regularly feed on assorted scraps and refuse pitched or pumped overboard.

Fulmars are tubenoses; they share with the albatross a common enlarged beak profile. They nest on eastern North Pacific islands far distant from their foraging locations off Washington's coast.

Only a small fraction of the larger populations of shearwaters and fulmars ever occur within the Strait of Juan de Fuca or Puget Sound. The few that do occasionally feed here might be subject to some oil contamination should they attempt to feed or roost in the presence of an oil slick. The pumping of bilge oil off the outer coast presents a greater threat to these species than does a spill within the waters of the Sound.

*Light color phase of northern fulmar*

### Sooty Shearwater
*Puffinus griseus*

Length 41 cm (16 in)
Wingspread 110 cm (43 in)

**Status and Distribution**  An abundant migrant off Washington's coast, these birds occasionally occur within Puget Sound at various times of the year (Jewett et al., 1953). From April to November they work the open coastal waters, then return to their breeding grounds far to the south near Cape Horn and New Zealand.

Fall storms will push these birds into Puget Sound as far as Deception Pass, along Smith Island, and off Point Roberts.

**Food and Critical Habitat**  These birds feed on squids, sand lances, and anchovies. As they wander into Puget Sound they feed in open channels, and may fly as a group searching for schools of fish.

### Short-tailed Shearwater
*Puffinus tenuirostris*

Length 41 cm (16 in)
Wingspread 100 cm (39 in)

**Status and Distribution**  Short-tailed shearwaters are occasional visitors to the Strait of Juan de Fuca and Puget Sound. They are found off the Washington coast in varying numbers in most years. There are fall records for this species off Seattle and along The Narrows near Tacoma (Jewett et al., 1953).

**Food and Critical Habitat**  These birds seek small crustaceans—such as euphausiids, small fish, and squids—while working the open waters. They also scavenge from fishing boats.

### Northern Fulmar
*Fulmarus glacialis*

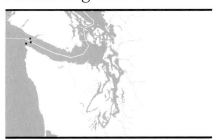

Length 46 cm (18 in)
Wingspread 108 cm (42 in)

**Status and Distribution**  These birds are common winter visitors off the outer coast from early October until April, but are less common through the summer months. They enter the Strait of Juan de Fuca irregularly.

**Food and Critical Habitat**  Fulmars are pelagic scavengers that readily feed on wastes discarded from fishing vessels. They also consume oil that occurs from natural seepage along with assorted fish, squids, and small crustaceans near the surface.

# Storm Petrels
## *Hydrobatidae*

Storm petrels are blackbird-sized birds imbued with myth and prominent in the folklore of the sea. They have a habit of patting the water and dipping their feet as they hover above the ocean's surface. This may have inspired their name, as petrel is thought to be a diminutive of "Saint Peter," who—legend has it—walked on water. Another name given these birds is "Mother Carey's chickens," derived from "Mata Cara," an incantation to the divine virgin given by seamen caught in violent storms. When a petrel appeared on the lee side of a ship during a storm, it was considered a signal that the prayer had been heard.

There are two species of storm petrels that breed on the islands off Washington's coast and occasionally enter the Strait of Juan de Fuca and Puget Sound. Like some of the smaller alcids, fork-tailed and Leach's storm petrels nest in burrows and are nocturnal in their activities when breeding. This strategy helps them avoid predation by gulls, for these little birds hobble helplessly on land and are easy prey for an alert avian predator in daylight. The storm petrel's legs are barely strong enough to paddle about in the water; on land they shuffle along, bent over, using their wings to aid their movements.

Ships often provide sustenance for these birds, and they do not hesitate to snatch scraps from a ship's wake. As a rule, however, they consume crustaceans, small fish, and squids.

Bilge oil released off Washington's coast can, for a period of time, contaminate their feeding grounds but a larger threat to petrel populations is human activity on their breeding islands.

# Leach's Storm Petrel
*Oceanodroma leucorhoa*

Length 19 cm (7.5 in)
Wingspread 48 cm (19 in)

**Status and Distribution**    A breeding bird on Tatoosh and other islands off the Washington coast, sighting records suggest that this petrel occurs within Puget Sound most often during winter months (Jewett et al., 1953). It is a very unusual visitor in the Sound, but it has been sighted as far south as The Narrows at Tacoma.

**Food and Critical Habitat**    These birds move well off shore from their breeding islands to forage. They feed on small fish, squids, and euphausiids that live in offshore waters, which are slightly warmer than the nearshore waters exploited by fork-tailed petrels (Paulson, 1980). When opportunity permits they forage on the wastes left by feeding whales.

Offshore breeding islands are critical to the presence of this and other species of marine birds in the Strait of Juan de Fuca and Puget Sound. This petrel requires substrate that is soft enough that the bird can use its beak to excavate a burrow, sometimes as deep as a meter. In these burrows, or in rock cavities, the petrel finds protection to raise its single youngster.

# Fork-tailed Storm Petrel
*Oceanodroma furcata*

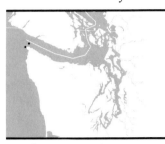

Length 19 cm (7.5 in)
Wingspread 46 cm (18 in)

**Status and Distribution**    A breeding bird on Tatoosh Island, this petrel feeds well off shore and only rarely ventures into the Strait of Juan de Fuca (Manuwal et al., 1979).

**Food and Critical Habitat**    These birds search the offshore open waters for shrimps and small fish. Washington's coastal islands, which have substrate that permits burrowing, are critical breeding habitat for this species. The foraging birds that occur within the Strait of Juan de Fuca likely originate from these islands.

*Leach's petrels (left) off Tatoosh Island.
Fork-tailed petrel (right) at entrance
to the Strait of Juan de Fuca*

# Pelicans
*Pelecanidae*

Our northern outer coast waters occasionally host pelican patrols. Moving in a long sustained sail just seaward of the intertidal zone, they look rather like miniature pterodactyls, wings alternately beating then set for gliding. Even while heavy winds stir a froth from along the surf, the brown pelicans steer a steady course over the fishing beds. One of the great ungainly looking birds turns on its wing, circles slowly over the water, then plunges for a fish.

As it throws its body headlong into the turbulent waters, I marvel at this bird's skeletal structure, which absorbs the shock of these dives over and over again, day after day. Beneath the bird's skin are numerous air sacs, which give the body buoyancy. The pelican pops back immediately to the surface, with a fish it has scooped up in the dip-net pouch of its beak.

Along the Pacific Coast, the pelican's population has declined. Pesticides in their food appear to be the chief cause (Blus et al., 1974). They cause the shell of pelican's eggs to become thin and fragile, drastically reducing successful hatching rates—the same fate that befell the peregrine falcon. This problem has been documented in birds that nested on islands off the California coast. Whether marine birds that breed in more remote regions of the continent are similarly affected is unknown, however. The ultimate effect of toxicants in the marine environment may be years in the measuring.

## Brown Pelican
*Pelecanus occidentalis*

Length 105 cm (41 in)
Wingspread 230 cm (90 in)

**Status and Distribution**  The brown pelican wanders along Washington's outer coast following the spring/summer breeding season, and makes rare appearances in the Strait of Juan de Fuca.

**Food and Critical Habitat**  This majestic bird fishes the shallow waters off the coast and around islands for a variety of fish, including herring and smelts.

## White Pelican
*Pelecanus erythrorhynchos*

Length 128 cm (50 in)
Wingspread 282 cm (110 in)

**Status and Distribution**  Formerly a breeding bird in Eastern Washington, the white pelican is a spring and fall migrant that rarely occurs in Puget Sound. There are records, however, for both late spring and fall sightings: at Dungeness Bay in May 1976, in the Nisqually estuary in June 1978, and in Budd Inlet in October 1978 (Gardner, 1979).

**Food and Critical Habitat**  This pelican, unlike the brown pelican that dives from the air to snatch its underwater prey, feeds on the surface where fish school. It thrusts its head deep into the water, scooping up a wide variety of fish from both fresh and salt water.

The white pelican requires isolated areas where it may retreat to rest. Like all species that depend on the marine habitat it has suffered from intrusion by humans. Whether we personally see one of the few wanderers that enter the Sound is not nearly as important as knowing that this impressive creature is still aloft and healthy somewhere in those parts of our world that remain pristine.

# Cormorants
## *Phalacrocoracidae*

In the water, with only my head bobbing on the surface, I can reach an intimacy with marine birds not achieved when viewing from land or boat. Letting currents sweep me around the edges of offshore rocks at the south end of Lopez Island, I appear to the birds to be just another sea mammal. Guillemots pull down through the surface close enough for me to see their white wing patches contrasted against the gloom of deep water. Sliding over a tangle of floating kelp I drop into a narrow chamber between the beds and the abrupt cliffs.

A pair of pelagic cormorants, standing sentry at their nest, pay me little notice. The male preens contentedly in the warm sun, his blue eye partially lidded. Over the flat calm waters other cormorants approach from their fishing grounds. A few meters from the rock they pull up, rising almost perpendicularly, to land on narrow ledges washed white with centuries of use. Some birds are there only to rest and dry their wings, others to brood young. Between some parents I can see the fuzzy, wobbly-necked, open-mouthed new generation.

The three representatives of the cormorant family found in the Puget Sound region, the double-crested, Brandt's, and pelagic cormorants, are highly specialized fishing birds. Their evolutionary lines have followed those of other families of marine birds and yet they possess some qualities uniquely their own. The cormorant's serrated and hooked bill, for example, is similar to the merganser's, and is used with efficiency in capturing herring, blennies, sand lances, and sculpins. Like diving ducks and loons they propel their streamlined bodies beneath the water by rapidly paddling their feet. Cormorants, however, possess feet with three webbed surfaces; ducks and loons have but two. Cormorants on the other hand do not share the water repellent plumage possessed by other waterfowl and must leave the water periodically to "dry out."

Different feeding and nesting preferences allow cormorants to reduce competition among the species for suitable habitat. Because of size differences, different species feed on a wide range of prey. Variations in nesting requirements and habits space the populations on Washington's coast. Double-crested cormorants breed almost exclusively in early May. Brandt's cormorants begin nesting at the end of May, and build nests on rocky slopes while the double-crested cormorants are feeding their rapidly developing young on the ground above (Jewett et al., 1953). The cliff-ledge-

*Pair of Brandt's cormorants*

nesting pelagic cormorants time nest construction and egg laying activities between the other two. This phasing of breeding reduces competition for food by shortening the periods when two or more nesting populations are feeding young at the same time.

My observations suggest that when the "real estate" is available, the earlier nesting pelagic cormorants show a preference for southern exposure in locating their nests. There are obvious solar heating advantages in these locations and their featherless, dark-skinned hatchlings make good use of it. Roosting too is done on the southerly portions of island cliffs. Such locations are extremely important to the welfare of these birds, which need sites to rest out of water and dry out their feathers.

Although all three species winter in Puget Sound, only the double-crested and pelagic cormorants nest here in substantial numbers. The Brandt's cormorant nests only on the outer coast.

Cormorants can normally keep marauding eagles, gulls, crows, and ravens at bay while brooding their eggs and young. They use size and steep nesting areas to their advantage. They do not stand fast in the face of human intrusion, however. Boaters approaching the colonies send adults into flight, leaving eggs and young exposed to predation and chilling.

Because these are diving birds, they are particularly vulnerable to the effects of oil spilled in their fishing waters. Because large numbers of pelagic and double-crested cormorants depend upon Puget Sound throughout the year, the population is at risk as well as individual birds.

# Double-crested Cormorant
*Phalacrocorax auritus*

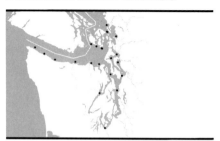

Length 69 cm (27 in)
Wingspread 128 cm (50 in)

**Status and Distribution** This species is found year-round in the San Juan Islands, the Strait of Juan de Fuca, and Puget Sound. It is perhaps the most common cormorant in the Sound, breeding in the Canadian Gulf Islands and the American San Juan Islands.

There are breeding colonies on Mandarte Island (some 700 birds), Rose Islets (160 birds), and Ballingal (140 cormorants) in the Gulf Islands. Within the Strait of Juan de Fuca and the San Juan Islands it is estimated that there are about 180 breeding pairs (Gardner, 1979). Colville Island hosts an important colony of 50 birds. Lummi and Viti Rocks provide breeding habitat for comparable numbers.

**Food and Critical Habitat** These birds are capable divers, going as deep as 20 meters to feed on sticklebacks, cabezons, and other sculpins. Occasionally they eat salmon fingerlings, but their principal prey species are not considered to be economically important.

Double-crested cormorants favor estuarine waters for feeding. They frequently move into protected bays, where one can see them perched on docks and pilings to dry out and preen their plumage. To breed, however, they move where there are rocky crests upon which to build their nests.

# Brandt's Cormorant
*Phalacrocorax penicillatus*

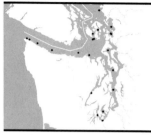

Length 74 cm (29 in)
Wingspread 128 cm (50 in)

**Status and Distribution** A common winter resident throughout Puget Sound, this bird occasionally breeds at the western end of the Strait of Juan de Fuca.

**Food and Critical Habitat** Like the other cormorants, the Brandt's seeks fish and will often feed on small schools of herring in the deep waters of harbors and entrance channels, and in tide-rip areas in company with arctic loons, rhinoceros auklets, and murres (Paulson, 1980). A deep diver, this bird occasionally reaches depths of 50 meters when pursuing its prey, but also fishes the shallow waters of estuaries and over reefs.

The nesting conditions required by the Brandt's cormorant include islands with sloping to flat tops, where it constructs nests of twigs lined with grass and seaweed. It is especially sensitive to human activity near nesting colonies. Isolated or generally undisturbed locations are also needed for resting and drying feathers.

*Profiles of nesting pelagic cormorants on Colville Island*

# Pelagic Cormorant
## *Phalacrocorax pelagicus*

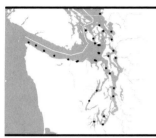

Length 56 cm (22 in)
Wingspread 103 cm (40 in)

**Status and Distribution** A permanent resident and breeding bird, this is perhaps the most widely distributed of the cormorants occurring within Puget Sound. Compared with counts of this species made early in this century (Jewett et al., 1953), 1979–80 resident numbers suggest a decline of the pelagic cormorant.

There are active nesting aggregations of this species on Mandarte, Bare, and Gabriola Islands in Canadian waters. In American waters, Colville Island has an important breeding population of 44 pairs. Protection and Smith Islands and Port Angeles Harbor also host significant numbers of nesting birds. Throughout northern Puget Sound and the Strait there is an estimated total breeding population of about 950 pairs of birds (Manuwal et al., 1979).

**Food and Critical Habitat** Pelagic cormorants feed on herring, a wide range of bottomfish, and crustaceans. These versatile feeders exploit various waters, particularly those near steep rocky cliffs where they nest and roost. They begin laying eggs in June and often form colonies that are small compared with other cormorants nesting on the coast.

*Pair of pelagic cormorants*
*in breeding plumage*

# Herons
## *Ardeidae*

One winter day in 1979 I joined a group of people representing resource agencies and conservation organizations to discuss establishment of an estuarine sanctuary near Padilla Bay. I remember the day for two reasons. First there was the excitement we shared over the possibility of preserving one of the most important wintering areas in North America for species of waterfowl, shorebirds, and raptors. The second memorable element of this out-of-doors meeting was that we were surrounded by the creatures that inspired our commitment. While maps were produced and plans developed, we were constantly pulling our heads from the huddle to follow some new movement or find the source of a curious call that had drifted toward us from the bay.

One of the major players on the bay that day was a great blue heron that had speared an enormous perch in the shallows off shore. Our discussions were suspended as we watched the bird handle its catch. After spearing the fish it secured its mandibles around the fish's head. From a distance it appeared an impossible task for the heron to swallow the fish, which was longer than the bird's head. Yet bit by bit, shifting its long neck like a Balinese dancer, the heron moved its meal into and down its throat. At one point the bird appeared to have two heads. Then it seemed the fish was stuck as the bird rested. It took 20 minutes from the time the fish disappeared, becoming a bulge moving down that long neck, until it finally reached its digestive destiny. When it was all over, the heron looked as gaunt and hungry as before.

Herons move from freshwater rivers, lakes, and ponds to shallow waters of beaches and mudflats to hunt. Along salt marshes the birds fish, and in the nearby grassy areas they prey on small mammals. In these habitats they patiently stalk voles. Poised, statue-like, they wait until the tiny animal emerges from its grassy tunnel and then spear it with the speed of a striking snake. They employ a similar strategy when stalking fish in the shallow pools that are formed along the beaches at low tide.

Herons have taken the long-legged, long-necked route to the exploitation of food resources in shallow water habitats. They can successfully fish waters more than a half meter deep. They also fish off shore, using kelp beds as a platform from which to spot and secure food. Although the water here may be ten or more meters deep, smaller fish live close to the surface using the thick kelp for cover. When the mat shifts in the currents, exposing the prey, the heron is waiting.

The great blue is the only representative of the heron family commonly found on Puget Sound. Other members, like the bittern, occasionally wander to its edges but the Sound's waters are not their principal habitat.

Although this graceful species is still harassed and shot illegally it is not particularly susceptible to oiling. Like other species fishing in estuaries, herons are exposed to toxins accumulating here from direct dumping or upstream runoff.

## Great Blue Heron
*Ardea herodias*

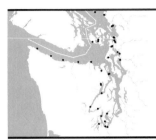

Length 97 cm (38 in)
Wingspread 179 cm (70 in)

**Status and Distribution**    The great
blue heron is a year-round resident
throughout much of Puget Sound. Its
breeding colonies are adjacent to both
fresh- and saltwater locations. There
are nesting colonies at Samish Island
(over 100 pairs), Coronet Bay, Camano
Island, Mats Mats Bay, Bolton and
Tahuya Peninsulas on Hood Canal, and
Bainbridge Island. At low tide, large
feeding aggregations can be found in
Padilla and Bellingham Bays and at the
mouth of the Nisqually River.

**Food and Critical Habitat**    These
birds are versatile and opportunistic
feeders in Puget Sound and along the
Strait of Juan de Fuca. With their long
legs they can wade in waters along sand
and mud beaches to stab perch, sculpins, starry flounders, and sanddabs.
They are particularly fond of fishing
the shallow pools that often contain
prey stranded by the low tide.

*Heron downing a perch at Padilla Bay*

# Swans, Geese, and Ducks
## *Anatidae*

Most of us who travel Interstate 5 from Olympia to Bellingham give scant thought to the reservoir of life only minutes to the west. We tend to race from one destination to the next directed by datebooks and restricted by watches. Many years ago I made a detour, however, to gaze out over the water and mudflats facing Fir Island and Saratoga passage. Waterfowl were assembled in the tens of thousands. A clamorous throng of snow geese rose up to the edges of black clouds in a detonation of light. Scythe-winged teal dropped abruptly from some invisible sky lane to slip smoothly into a remote slough. At the island's northern edges, a thousand pintails paddled and poked in the shallow puddles or waddled at the water's edge, nervously eyeing the silhouette of a peregrine falcon atop a rock ledge.

Of the seven "tribes" of Anatidae that occur in North America all except the whistling ducks are represented in Puget Sound: swans and geese, perching ducks, dabbling ducks, pochards, sea ducks, and eiders. Swans, and particularly geese, compose one major tribe. Both the trumpeter and whistling swans "tip up" their tails from the surface as they stretch their long necks down into the water to reach the vegetation below. The larger trumpeter swan occasionally feeds in salt water, and the whistler does so regularly. Both species fly to open fields and lakes inland from the mouth of the Skagit River to feed on emergent plants.

Snow geese regularly move along saltwater margins of Skagit Bay to Port Susan and Livingston Bays when not feeding in nearby fields. The brant, on the other hand, normally restrict their feeding to the bays, shallows, and beaches where eelgrass is abundant, using their serrated mandibles as effective "clippers." When winter storms wash the grasses to the beach the brant feed there.

Members of this group do not show sexually dimorphic plumage patterns—males and females have the same coloring. They are known for the fidelity of their pair bonds. The pair of whistling swans gliding in slow motion above Wiley Slough will probably remain together until one of them dies.

Perching ducks compose the next tribe. They are for the most part tropical and subtropical, and our sole representative of this group is the wood duck. It is a freshwater species and does not normally occur on salt water at any time. It does occasionally nest close to salt water, particularly where ponds form along a river delta and borders of cottonwoods pro-

vide cavities where it can brood eggs and young.

Dabbling ducks are more completely represented on the Sound as a tribe. They are characterized by their habit of feeding from surface or shallow waters with their tails up and heads down, and by their ability to take off abruptly from both water and land. They walk reasonably well on land, and can forage far up on the shores of bays and inlets as well as in open fields. As a rule they are sexually dimorphic, showing distinct plumage differences between the adult males and females.

Although most surface feeders prefer fresh to salt water, mallards, pintails, and American wigeons winter along the edges of the Sound in large numbers. Shovelers, gadwals, European wigeons, and green-winged teals come here in fewer numbers.

The fifth tribe, the pochards, is made up of diving ducks. Their legs are set farther back on their bodies than those of the surface feeding ducks. This anatomical arrangement makes them awkward walkers, but it does account for their capacity to dive. When taking flight these ducks make a foot-slapping run over the surface. Pochards also have longer toes and broader webs, which contribute to their effectiveness underwater. The stout, heavy bills of most of these ducks are essential for foraging underwater.

Within the bays of the Sound scaups are by far the most common of the pochards. Canvasbacks are much less numerous and prefer the northern portions of Puget Sound.

The sea duck tribe, many of which breed in the Arctic and winter in Washington's marine waterways, feed predominately upon animal matter. Like the pochards, their legs are situated well back on the body, enabling them to dive deeply and maneuver effectively underwater. Some sea ducks, like the oldsquaw, are inclined to work the deeper channels for food and remain there to rest on the surface.

Although the eiders rarely venture into Puget Sound, the balance of this tribe's North American members do occur here at some time of the year. Harlequins, Barrow's goldeneyes, hooded and common mergansers breed in Washington far inland from the salt water. The best represented of these ducks are buffleheads and white-winged and surf scoters. As a rule, they are more often heard than seen from land's edge. The whistling whir of surf scoter's wings as they take off or fly past is a common sound on bays and beaches from late summer to the following spring. Oldsquaws, on the other hand, are normally seen far

*Pair of hooded mergansers
at Mackaye Harbor, Lopez Island*

off shore and though they are among the most numerous sea ducks worldwide, their numbers in Puget Sound are small.

Puget Sound's single representative of the stiff-tailed tribe is the ruddy duck. When the male bristles its tail, it is nearly at right angles to the rest of its stubby body, an unmistakable identifying characteristic. Its legs are situated well back on the body, making it nearly helpless on land. These heavy-billed little ducks winter throughout the Sound in small groups of six or eight birds. Their food is predominately vegetable matter, which is retrieved in shallow dives.

From the foregoing discussion one can begin to recognize a simple feeding zonation for the family Anatidae. Whistling swans, snow geese, and dabbling ducks forage on shore and sluice the mud and shallow waters for aquatic plants. Within and immediately beyond the intertidal zone, pochards dive for molluscs and crustaceans. They are often joined by the sea ducks, which extend their foraging range out to the deep channels. Among the latter group the scoters plunge only a few meters down to feed from mussel beds in the intertidal, while oldsquaws exploit the resources from deeper waters.

Besides the ubiquitous gulls, the members of this family are probably among the best known of the region's marine birds. They have important economic value as well. Every year people spend millions of dollars hunting, photographing, and watching them, so it is not surprising that there is considerable public concern for their welfare. The most serious threat to their population is loss of habitat to which their survival is inextricably linked. These problems are discussed further under the species accounts.

Oil spills represent a serious potential danger to marine ducks. When they dive into oil-covered waters their plumage becomes mired with oil. Sea ducks are most affected by oil spills, although some are more vulnerable than others, depending on their feeding, flocking, and resting habits. Sea ducks that feed and rest in flocks on the water's surface expose large numbers of birds to a single oil spill. They are more vulnerable as a population than those that disperse.

The surf scoter is particularly sensitive to oil spills; a sizeable portion of its Pacific population winters in Puget Sound. Likewise populations of black scoters, Barrow's goldeneyes, harlequins, and greater scaup face serious impact from spills. Perhaps as many as 100,000 brant utilize Puget Sound as a feeding and staging area prior to flying north to breed. These birds flock in Fidalgo, Samish, and Padilla Bays, and are especially vulnerable to any oil contamination in that vicinity.

It should be further noted that estuaries and adjacent marshes are catchalls for toxic wastes washed from the interior. These areas are critical to the welfare of waterfowl, and toxic chemicals that accumulate there eventually are cycled into their diets.

## Whistling Swan
### *Cygnus columbianus*

Length 92 cm (36 in)
Wingspread 218 cm (85 in)

**Status and Distribution** Whistling swans are common winter migrants on Puget Sound as well as in freshwater habitats. Some birds remain throughout the winter. They appear by late October and remain into March, concentrating along the Skagit (approximately 200 birds winter here) and Nooksack River estuaries. The Nisqually Delta also hosts whistling swans.

**Food and Critical Habitat** Favoring leaves, roots, stems, and tubers of aquatic plants as well as waste crops, this species moves back and forth from estuaries to fresh water and agricultural fields of the interior Puget Sound basin. In brackish waters they also eat animal matter, mostly molluscs.

## Trumpeter Swan
### *Cygnus buccinator*

Length 115 cm (45 in)
Wingspread 244 cm (95 in)

**Status and Distribution** Only rarely seen on salt water, the trumpeter swan is a late fall and winter resident on fresh water and along the northern Puget Sound uplands. With a present population of nearly 300 birds, its comeback from near extinction in Washington less than 30 years ago is considered a success story. With continued encroachment on its habitat, however, its future in Washington is not secure, and it must still be judged a threatened species. The major concentrations of trumpeters are found along Barney Slough and on Clear Lake east of Mount Vernon.

**Food and Critical Habitat** Flying, swimming, walking, or standing along the water's edge, trumpeter swans are among the most impressive of northwest birds. They weigh up to 12 kg (26 lbs) and stand on pads up to 18 cm (7 in) across. They feed on grasses and waste crops in open fields, stems, tubers, roots, seeds of freshwater plants, and some animal matter, including fish, molluscs, and insects.

These swans usually restrict their movements to and from freshwater locations on northern Puget Sound, but when severe winters freeze fresh waters the marine shoreline becomes considerably important to this species. With this in mind, Skagit Bay should be considered an important reserve habitat for those swans.

Evidence from swans autopsied by the Washington State Department of Game show that some of these birds ingest lethal amounts of lead shot as they filter food from the sediments of Clear Lake, Barney Slough, and Beaver Lake. A management policy that would separate existing and potential swan feeding areas from intensive hunting locations where shot accumulates would resolve this problem. Requiring hunters to use only lead-iron shot (which is less lethal when ingested) in swan feeding locations would also benefit these birds (Finley and Dieter, 1978).

*Whistling swans at Skagit Delta*

# Canada Goose
## *Branta canadensis*

Length 64 cm (25 in)
Wingspread 174 cm (68 in)

**Status and Distribution**  The Canada goose is an uncommon winter resident and migrant in saltwater habitats on Puget Sound. Compared to the numbers on the outer Washington coast and east of the Cascades, very few of this species occur on the Sound although in the spring and summer they breed on the freshwater lakes nearby. Their numbers appear stable from year to year.

Important marine feeding and resting areas in Puget Sound include the shallow and protected bays at Dungeness and Port Gamble, Skagit Bay, and along the Nisqually Flats. Strawberry Bay on Cypress Island also hosts this species.

The resident Canada goose is the large "western" race, and along with migrant races—including the "dusky," "Vancouver," and "cackling"—only rarely strays into the Sound. It is more common on the outer coast (Paulson, 1980).

**Food and Critical Habitat**  These birds prefer vegetable matter and forage on mudflats, along salt marshes, and in estuaries feeding on reeds, eelgrass, and sea lettuce. They commonly feed on grain in the stubble fields adjacent to beaches.

*Canadian geese along Skagit Delta*

# Brant
## *Branta bernicla*

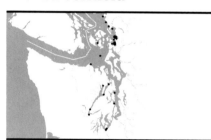

Length 44 cm (17 in)
Wingspread 123 cm (48 in)

**Status and Distribution**     A spring and fall migrant and winter resident along the Strait of Juan de Fuca, Hood Canal, and Puget Sound, brant are most numerous from September to November and from February into May. Fidalgo, Padilla, and Samish Bays are vital to the welfare of this species in this region. Spring population counts made in these locations during the early 1970s averaged more than 30,000 brant (Gardner, 1979). A large share of the Pacific coast population of this species (125,000–150,000 brant) may use these bays during the spring to restore their energy before moving north to the Arctic Circle to breed.

Smaller concentrations of brant also occur in Dungeness Bay and along Hood Canal at the mouths of the Skokomish and Dosewallips Rivers. Dabob Bay and the waters around Belfair (Lynch Cove) are also important. The Nisqually Flats provide feeding habitat for brant as do the bays and inlets near Harper. Farther north, Useless and Dugualla Bays on Whidbey Island are important, as is Drayton Harbor on the eastern side of Sinclair Island. Smith Island, Lummi and Birch Bays, and the northwestern edges of Bellingham Bay are also used by brant. Small flocks fly into the San Juan Islands in early spring to feed, pick up gravel, and rest along the beaches.

It should be noted that from 1973 to 1974 numbers of brant taken by hunters in the region declined by more than 50 percent (4,500 birds taken in 1973 and only 2,200 birds in 1974). The 1977 bag total was only 1,740. At the same time the number of hunters in the field increased. Although bag checks are by no means systematic they do show a population decline and should be considered indicators of the species' status.

It is also notable that total numbers of brant wintering on these waters have declined over the last decade. Current levels of 8,000–9,000 birds are far below a wintering population that once numbered over 30,000. The decline is due in part to an apparent shift away from this region to other wintering locations in Baja California.

**Food and Critical Habitat**  This little goose is dependent on eelgrass and sea lettuce. Its very survival here is closely linked to the presence of this food source. Gravel beaches with little disturbance permit the birds to walk the shore to feed, rest, and secure small stones necessary for the processing of their food.

Unfortunately, the most important wintering areas for brant are close to waters where there is intensive shipping activity and oil refineries. This creates potential threat of oiling for this species. Spills drifting into Padilla and Samish Bays would contaminate not only the birds but the eelgrass beds as well. An additional problem in these areas is that cordgrass (*spartina* sp.) is spreading slowly from its original planting and displacing plant species favored by brant.

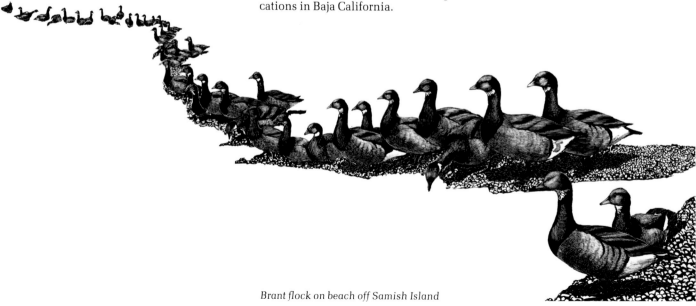

*Brant flock on beach off Samish Island*

*Snow geese along the
north fork of the Skagit River*

## Snow Goose
*Chen caerulescens*

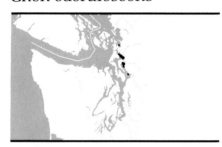

Length 49 cm (19 in)
Wingspread 151 cm (59 in)

**Status and Distribution**   Snow geese
are common fall and spring migrants
and winter residents from October into
April along the western edges of northern
Puget Sound. Skagit Flats and Skagit
and Port Susan Bays are of particular
importance to wintering flocks.
Within these regions the snow geese
settle into Livingston Bay, along Warm
Beach, and the Stillaguamish Delta.
They occasionally utilize the Nisqually
Delta.

The greatest concentrations of geese
winter here from the middle of December
into February. After several years of
decline during the mid- and late 1970s,
the populations of snow geese in northern
Puget Sound reached more than
29,000 birds for the winter of 1979–80
(Dept. of Game, 1980). This population
is up from a long-term average in the
area of 21,000 geese. Because of reproduction
success, the region hosted
more than 40,000 of this species in the
winter of 1981–82. It has been estimated
that of this total 8,400 were
taken or crippled by hunters in the
1981 season.

**Food and Critical Habitat**       Snow
geese feed on bullrushes (roots and rhizomes),
sea lettuce, eelgrass, sedges,
and arrowgrass of the salt marshes.
They also eat waste crops and new
shoots in agricultural fields.

Salt marshes are enormously important
to this area's population of wintering
geese. The filling of wetlands and
gradual loss of eelgrass and bullrush
beds in shallow bays will continue to
affect the condition of the flocks. In
Port Susan Bay the presence of hybrid
cordgrass has the potential to displace
the highly productive bullrush marsh,
which is a favored feeding area of the
snow goose (Parker and Aberle, 1977).

A more obvious impact on these
geese is harassment by people flying
small airplanes over the flocks (*Seattle
Times*, 1981). I have on occasion
watched single planes make repeated
passes over flocks sending them into
panicked flight away from their feeding
areas. Indeed, these flights have been
frequent enough to cause the birds to
stop feeding and begin making alarm
calls at the mere sound of an approaching
plane.

It appears that the major portion of
snow geese that winter here and on the
Fraser River Delta outside of Vancouver,
British Columbia breed on Wrangell
Island in Siberia. Periodic declines
in goose populations attributed to nesting
failures due to poor weather conditions
are compounded by continued
encroachment on wintering habitat and
human activity that disrupts normal
feeding and resting. To mitigate these
impacts, important habitat areas for
this species should be considered inviolable
outside of the hunting season.

## Emperor Goose
*Chen canagica*

Length 46 cm (18 in)
Wingspread 136 cm (53 in)

**Status and Distribution**   The emperor
goose is not seen regularly every year in
the Sound, but it is a rare winter visitor
that has been seen in a wide range of locations
(Paulson, 1980).

**Food and Critical Habitat**   A sea loving
goose, this lovely patterned bird is
usually vegetarian. Eelgrass and sea lettuce
are considerably important to its
diet, although it consumes molluscs
and crustaceans as well.

## White-fronted Goose
*Anser albifrons*

Length 51 cm (20 in)
Wingspread 154 cm (60 in)

## Mallard
*Anas platyrhnchos*

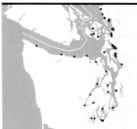

Length 41 cm (16 in)
Wingspread 92 cm (36 in)

**Status and Distribution**  These birds are common spring migrants along Washington's outer coast from April to mid-May, and in the fall from September to October. White-fronted geese occasionally winter within the Sound and along the Strait of Juan de Fuca. They are seen infrequently at Dungeness and Skagit Bays.

**Food and Critical Habitat**  The marine food choices of the white-fronted goose are primarily vegetable, and include sea lettuce, eelgrass, and sedges taken in or near salt marshes, a favored habitat. They forage in estuarine waters and along tidal flats.

**Status and Distribution**  An abundant year-round resident of Puget Sound, a November peak of mallards has averaged about 40,000 birds over 19 years, concentrated around Port Susan, Skagit, Padilla, and Samish Bays (Salo, 1975). An additional 5,000 mallards in the Snohomish River Delta indicates that these waters are also important for wintering birds. Farther north, the Nooksack River Delta and Bellingham Bays are also important as fall migration and wintering areas (6,000 mallards counted). To the west, Dungeness and Sequim Bays provide important sustenance to spring and winter migrants (Jeffrey, 1976). The Nisqually Delta is southern Puget Sound's most important wintering area for mallards (Mathematical Sciences Northwest, 1977).

**Food and Critical Habitat**  Although they prefer plant matter when feeding within the Sound, mallards also consume small crustaceans and molluscs. On salt water they are usually seen feeding in waters over mudflats, along sand and gravel shores, and in estuarine waters. They primarily breed along the edges of bodies of fresh water.

*White-fronted geese along Dungeness Spit*

# Pintail
*Anas acuta*

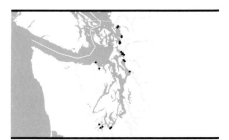

Length 47 cm (18.5 in)
Wingspread 90 cm (35 in)

**Status and Distribution** The pintail duck is an abundant winter resident on Puget Sound, with migratory flocks passing through in spring and fall. Among dabbling ducks, the pintail, green-winged teal, and American wigeon are the most common ducks within the salt marshes and estuaries of the Sound (Gardner, 1979).

Samish, Padilla, Skagit, and Port Susan Bays are areas where many pintails concentrate. Over 19 years, October and November populations have averaged 30,000 birds (Salo, 1975). The Nooksack estuary and Bellingham Bay host large numbers of pintails, and to the west Dungeness and Sequim Bays are equally important feeding areas. Nisqually Delta, Budd and Skookum Inlets, and Oakland Bay provide feeding and resting locations for migrating and wintering pintails in southern Puget Sound.

**Food and Critical Habitat** Although pintails feed on small molluscs and crustaceans when wintering on salt water, plant matter makes up most of their diet. They forage from the surface in shallow water along mudflats and beaches. Protected bays and estuaries, as well as adjacent salt marshes, provide resting places for these birds.

# Gadwall
*Anas strepera*

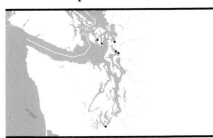

Length 37 cm (14.5 in)
Wingspread 90 cm (35 in)

**Status and Distribution** An uncommon winter visitor on salt waters of Puget Sound, the gadwall is more common in fresh water. The Nisqually Flats have small numbers of wintering gadwalls as do Mud and Fisherman's Bays on Lopez Island. Occasionally, they occur singly or in pairs in Padilla and Skagit Bays.

**Food and Critical Habitat** When in salt water this species prefers vegetable matter—algae, sea lettuce, eelgrass, and assorted sedges of the salt marsh.

In recent years the gadwall has increased in numbers to occupy shallow bays with fine and coarse sediment substrates. They rest on the waters and beaches of these bays.

# Green-winged Teal
*Anas crecca*

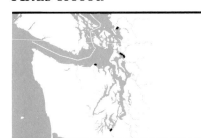

Length 27 cm (10.5 in)
Wingspread 62 cm (24 in)

**Status and Distribution** A common winter resident on Puget Sound, significant numbers of green-winged teals feed in Dungeness Bay (3,000 in January 1975) and the Skagit Delta (40,000 in 1978). The Nooksack and Nisqually Deltas occasionally host large numbers of teals (Gardner, 1979). Fidalgo Bay is used by wintering green-wings.

**Food and Critical Habitat** This small duck forages in bays and along tidal flats for vegetable matter including sedges and eelgrass. It is often found in company with mallards and pintails. It is also fond of feeding in the narrow channels of brackish water that lace the river deltas and occur along dikes.

*Pair of pintail ducks at Skagit Delta*

| Blue-winged Teal<br>*Anas discors* | American Wigeon<br>*Anas americana* | European Wigeon<br>*Anas penelope* |
|---|---|---|

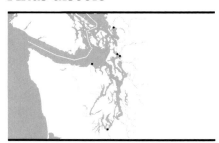

Length 28 cm (11 in)
Wingspread 62 cm (24 in)

Length 36 cm (14 in)
Wingspread 87 cm (34 in)

Length 35 cm (13.5 in)
Wingspread 82 cm (32 in)

**Status and Distribution** An uncommon spring and fall migrant on Puget Sound, blue-wings occasionally occupy the same locations favored by the green-winged teal.

**Food and Critical Habitat** This small surface feeder is primarily a vegetarian, eating seeds, sedges, and weeds. It also consumes some animal food from the shallow nearshore waters of salt marshes and estuaries.

**Status and Distribution** The American wigeon is an abundant winter resident on Puget Sound. The 19-year monthly average for the entire four-bay area around Samish, Padilla, Skagit and Port Susan Bays shows a high of 35,000–40,000 wigeons for the month of November (Salo, 1975). Dungeness Bay and Spit are also important: October counts of 36,000 of this species have been made here, and a January count found about half that number remaining (Gardner, 1979). Other areas important to this species are the Nooksack Delta, including Lummi and Bellingham Bays, and to the south, the Snohomish and Nisqually River Deltas.

**Food and Critical Habitat** Wigeons prefer vegetable matter when they are feeding in salt water, and dabble for sea lettuce, algae, and eelgrass. Although they forage in shallow waters over mud and fine sediments, they also regularly move to land to graze on grasses.

**Status and Distribution** A rare winter visitor, there are scattered records of this species occurring throughout Puget Sound. It is more common on fresh water, and is usually found as part of an aggregation of American wigeons.

**Food and Critical Habitat** A vegetarian, this surface-feeding duck occupies the same niche as the American wigeon. When foraging in shallow saltwater bays and flats, it feeds on algae and eelgrass.

# Northern Shoveler
## *Anas clypeata*

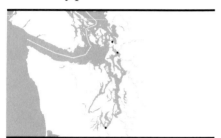

Length 36 cm (14 in)
Wingspread 79 cm (31 in)

**Status and Distribution**  The northern shoveler is a common winter resident on Puget Sound. Fidalgo Bay, with its backdrop of immense oil tankers, is a popular wintering habitat. Smaller numbers of these birds winter along the Nisqually Flats.

**Food and Critical Habitat**  In January, flocks of shovelers, sometimes numbering over 100 birds, gather at the edges of saltwater beaches to rest, preen, initiate courtship, and mate. They also use offshore waters to rest, secure from land-based predators. They feed on very small vegetable and animal matter, which they sluice from the sediment and water. In general, shovelers' feeding habitat overlaps with that of other important dabbling duck feeding areas.

# Ring-necked Duck
## *Aythya collaris*

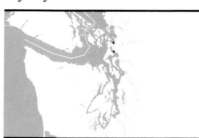

Length 31 cm (12 in)
Wingspread 72 cm (28 in)

**Status and Distribution**  A migrant and winter visitor to Puget Sound when its preferred freshwater habitat is frozen, the ring-necked duck is otherwise rare on salt water.

**Food and Critical Habitat**  When it occurs on salt water the ring-necked duck is most often found within tidal estuaries. It feeds on both vegetable and animal matter, foraging for algae and small molluscs, crustaceans, worms, and occasionally small fish.

# Redhead
## *Aythya americana*

Length 37 cm (14.5 in)
Wingspread 85 cm (33 in)

**Status and Distribution**  An uncommon wintering bird on Puget Sound, the redhead is a widespread migrant that prefers fresh water. This species breeds in Washington east of the Cascade Mountains.

**Food and Critical Habitat**  Primarily a vegetarian, this duck also consumes small quantities of animal matter. Redheads occupy the deeper waters of sheltered bays where they dive for food.

*Flock of shovelers at tide's edge in Fidalgo Bay*

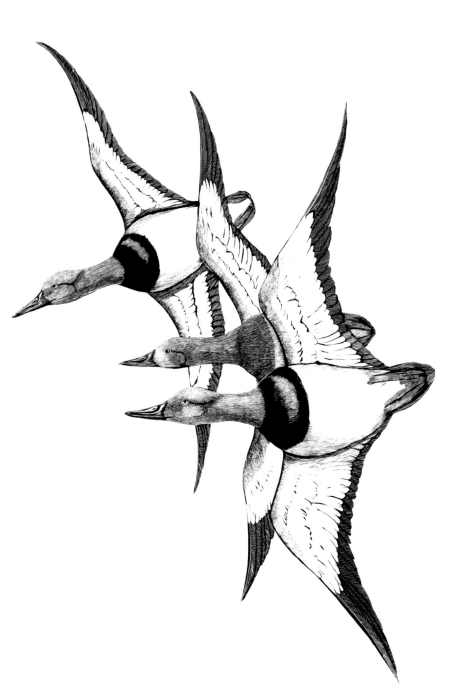

# Canvasback
*Aythya valisineria*

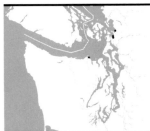

Length 38 cm (15 in)
Wingspread 87 cm (34 in)

**Status and Distribution** An uncommon winter resident on Puget Sound, this species has declined throughout much of its range. In northern Puget Sound, Padilla and Samish Bays are important wintering areas for the canvasback; 1,500 to 2,000 birds utilize these waters (Gardner, 1979). Dungeness Bay affords good feeding grounds for these birds.

To the south, the waters bordering Whidbey Island are important to wintering canvasbacks as are those within Elliott Bay and surrounding waters, the Nisqually Delta, and Henderson, Budd, Eld, Totten, and Skookum Inlets (Hesselbart and Hight, 1977).

**Food and Critical Habitat** This big duck feeds on eelgrass and other plants, and small fish and molluscs. It prefers the open waters of bays, estuaries, and harbors.

*Canvasback ducks off Bayview State Park, Padilla Bay*

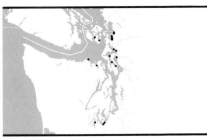

Greater scaups in Padilla Bay

## Greater Scaup
*Aythya marila*

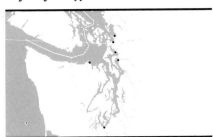

Length 33 cm (13 in)
Wingspread 79 cm (31 in)

**Status and Distribution** The greater scaup is a common migrant and winter resident throughout Puget Sound. In December, Bellingham Bay is used by large flocks of scaup. In Padilla Bay, migrating flocks of greater scaups average close to 10,000 birds in the fall (Gardner, 1981). The larger region including Padilla, Samish, Skagit, and Port Susan Bays, along with Saratoga Passage, have had maximum January counts of 38,000 of these ducks. Dungeness Bay has had April counts of 1,200 birds (Mathematical Sciences Northwest, 1977). Discovery and Elliott Bays also support significant numbers of greater scaup. Lopez Island hosts small wintering flocks of 25–100 birds in Mud and Fisherman's Bays.

**Food and Critical Habitat** These diving ducks work the shallows, as well as open deep-water bays along estuaries, looking for small molluscs, crustaceans, and assorted vegetable matter, including sea lettuce and eelgrass. Given the opportunity, scaups also eat herring spawn.

This species moves to shore to rest and clean and condition plumage to retain water repellency. They frequently mix with buffleheads and scoters in bays throughout the San Juan Islands.

## Lesser Scaup
*Aythya affinis*

Length 31 cm (12 in)
Wingspread 74 cm (29 in)

**Status and Distribution** A common migrant and winter resident on fresh water, the lesser scaup is not nearly as common as the greater scaup on salt water (Paulson, 1980). When in the bays of the San Juan Islands—such as Strawberry Bay on Cypress Island—or Puget Sound, they prefer the same habitat as the greater scaup and frequently join their flocks.

**Food and Critical Habitat** The diets of these birds vary, but like the larger greater scaup, they dive in shallow bays and estuaries for animal matter—crustaceans and molluscs—and move close to beaches to dabble for sea lettuce and eelgrass.

# Common Goldeneye
*Bucephala clangula*

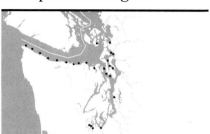

Length 33 cm (13 in)
Wingspread 79 cm (31 in)

**Status and Distribution** The common goldeneye is regularly seen as a migrant and winter resident from the middle of October to mid-April. It prefers sheltered waters and over an eight-year period this species' winter populations ranged from 3,000 to 16,500 birds (the average winter population was 5,700) concentrated in Admiralty Inlet, Saratoga Passage, and Port Susan, Padilla, and Skagit Bays (Mathematical Sciences Northwest, 1977).

Singly and in pairs they frequent the bays of the San Juan Islands and are common throughout the eastern edge of the Strait of Juan de Fuca and at times within Discovery Bay (Gardner, 1979 and Paulson, 1980). Along Hood Canal this species favors all the bays and estuaries. In southern Puget Sound, Budd, Eld, Totten, and Skookum Inlets support sizeable wintering flocks of goldeneyes.

**Food and Critical Habitat** Goldeneyes are strong divers and may go as deep as five meters searching for molluscs and crustaceans. On other occasions they work the waters near rocky and sandy beaches, stirring up the substrate with sweeping motions of their feet and dislodging small prey. Like scoters and scaup, goldeneyes gather at herring spawning locations to feed.

# Barrow's Goldeneye
*Bucephala islandica*

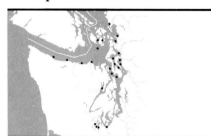

Length 33 cm (13 in)
Wingspread 79 cm (31 in)

**Status and Distribution** A fairly common migrant and winter resident from November to April, these ducks are less numerous than the common goldeneye. Like the common goldeneye, Barrow's goldeneyes operate in pairs or in small flocks of up to 30 birds. Admiralty Inlet, Skagit and Port Susan Bays, and Saratoga Passage are of particular importance to this species, as are Dungeness Bay (where there was a mid-1970s December count of 500 birds), and Skookum and Budd Inlets in southern Puget Sound (Gardner, 1981).

**Food and Critical Habitat** The Barrow's goldeneye prefers animal matter and dives for molluscs and crustaceans. It feeds in open waters off tidal flats and estuaries and in protected harbors. It also feeds on marine life found alongside pilings in marinas.

*Common Goldeneyes*

*Pair of Barrow's goldeneyes*

# Bufflehead
## *Bucephala albeola*

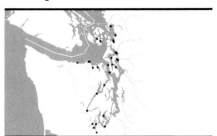

Length 26 cm (10 in)
Wingspread 62 cm (24 in)

**Status and Distribution** Common migrants and winter residents from late October into May, buffleheads are seen throughout Puget Sound. They are common in the eastern half of the Strait of Juan de Fuca; Dungeness Bay hosts up to 4,600 birds in December. The areas including Admiralty Inlet, Saratoga Passage, Port Susan, Skagit and Padilla Bays averaged some 7,650 birds during the winters over a six-year period in the 1970s (Gardner, 1981). The San Juan Archipelago has similar numbers of birds scattered within its sheltered bays and inlets: hundreds of buffleheads gather in Mud and Fisherman's Bays on Lopez Island. In southern Puget Sound, Budd, Eld, Totten and Skookum Inlets are used by hundreds of buffleheads.

**Food and Critical Habitat** A bird of open water within estuaries and shallow bays, this little duck dives to virtually all substrates to feed on small molluscs, crustaceans, and small fish. Quiet waters within inlets and bays are important to these animated ducks to initiate courtship displays. As early as February the males can be seen bobbing and skidding over the water's surface. With their irridescent head feathers flared and their bold black and white contour feathers set off against gray winter waters, they compete for the attentions of the comparatively drab females.

# Oldsquaw
## *Clangula hyemalis*

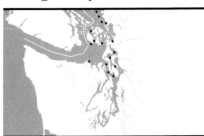

Length 38 cm (15 in)
Wingspread 77 cm (30 in)

**Status and Distribution** A locally common winter resident, the oldsquaw occurs on Puget Sound from November to May. This species is most common in the northern waters of Puget Sound, but uncommon south of Admiralty Inlet. The Strait of Georgia is especially important for feeding and resting oldsquaws, as are Admiralty Inlet, Saratoga Passage, and Skagit and Padilla Bays, where January populations averaged 450 birds over a seven-year period during the early 1960s (Gardner, 1979). Also of some importance is Dungeness Bay, which had a mid-1970s January count of 260 birds (Mathematical Sciences Northwest, 1977). The balance of the oldsquaws' wintering population is sprinkled throughout the channels of the San Juan Islands.

**Food and Critical Habitat** Oldsquaws favor animal food, including amphipods, mud crabs, and shrimps. Mussels are their favorite molluscs, and small fish prey includes sticklebacks and sculpins. They also eat herring spawn on occasion (Jewett et al., 1953) and some marine algae (Paulson, 1980).

A duck of the open-water habitat, the oldsquaw regularly plunges 20 meters or more to obtain food. Major entrance channels are important gathering locations for this species, as are waters off large estuaries and protected harbors (Gardner, 1979).

*Oldsquaws coming in to feed off Sandy Point*

# Harlequin Duck
*Histrionicus histrionicus*

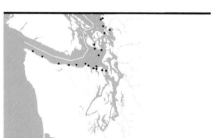

Length 31 cm (12 in)
Wingspread 67 cm (26 in)

**Status and Distribution** Residents of Washington, these stunning ducks breed inland along rivers and streams that offer sanctuary from human activity. The males gather on the Sound in small flocks in late summer and, after completing their brooding, the females bring their youngsters down the rivers to winter with the males from October to May of the following year.

Concentration areas include waters immediate to Marrowstone Island and along Protection Island, where molting birds gather to feed and rest in June and July. San Juan Channel and Smith Island waters also host harlequins as do those along Point White Horn, Birch Bay, and the shore waters between Bellingham and Blaine (Paulson, 1980). The Dungeness National Wildlife Refuge is very important to wintering harlequins.

**Food and Critical Habitat** Feeding almost entirely on animal matter, these birds dive for small crustaceans, assorted molluscs, and occasionally for fish. They prefer waters off rocky shores, although I have drifted along with feeding harlequins while skin diving and briefly followed their dives to eelgrass beds in waters only three meters deep. Here they caught small crabs, which they crushed with their stout beaks.

# White-winged Scoter
*Melanitta fusca*

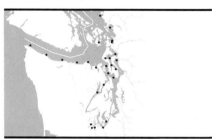

Length 41 cm (16 in)
Wingspread 97 cm (38 in)

**Status and Distribution** White-winged scoters are very common migrants and winter residents along the Strait of Juan de Fuca and within Puget Sound. Nonbreeding birds remain within the Sound through the summer. Their populations appear to be stable.

Over a seven-year period during the 1960s, winter populations of white-winged scoters in Admiralty Inlet, Saratoga Passage, Port Susan, Skagit, and Padilla Bays averaged 30,000 birds, with a high count of 50,000. Thousands of scoters winter in the waters of Penn Cove on Whidbey Island, in Discovery Bay, and along the Strait of Juan de Fuca (Gardner, 1979). San Juan Channel, Bellingham Bay, and Dungeness Bay are also important feeding locations for this species.

In Thatcher Pass, rafts of scoters feed in late winter and utilize more sheltered locations, including Mud and Fisherman's Bays on Lopez Island. In southern Puget Sound these birds winter off the mouth of the Nisqually River, and in Henderson, Budd, Eld, and Totten Inlets.

**Food and Critical Habitat** White-winged scoters eat crabs, clams, and mussels, and when the occasion permits they gather to feast on herring spawn. Diving over all substrates, they nevertheless prefer locations that support beds of shellfish, and frequently enter marinas where pilings support colonies of mussels.

# Surf Scoter
*Melanitta perspicillata*

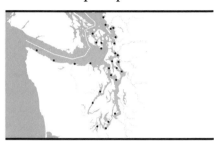

Length 36 cm (14 in)
Wingspread 85 cm (33 in)

**Status and Distribution** The surf scoter is a common migrant and winter resident from late August to May in the waters of the Strait of Juan de Fuca, the San Juan Islands, Puget Sound, and Hood Canal. Some birds remain here through the summer.

Surf scoter populations appear to be stable: Admiralty Inlet, Saratoga Passage, Port Susan, Padilla, and Skagit Bays have averaged 30,000 birds each winter over a seven-year period in the 1960s (Gardner, 1979). In winter, Bellingham Bay is used by this species, as are Mud Bay and San Juan Channel. In southern Puget Sound, Quartermaster Harbor on Vashon Island hosts hundreds of surf scoters during the fall and into the winter. Scattered flocks of surf scoters are found off McNeil Island where they feed in company with harbor seals. Dungeness Bay is also important to this species, as are waters off the Nisqually Delta.

**Food and Critical Habitat** Surf scoters seek molluscs and crustaceans in intermittent dives over rock, sand, and mud substrates of bays and channels. They are among the hardiest of ducks when it comes to braving the elements, and are often seen feeding on seething seas over reefs and off islands in Puget Sound. Like other marine ducks they rest on open water.

These birds often form feeding aggregations and sometimes submerge and surface as a group. Their courtship begins in late winter and they prefer calm, undisturbed waters for their displays.

*Single female harlequin duck joins males
off Marrowstone Island*

*"Squabbling" male surf scoters*

# Black Scoter
*Melanitta nigra*

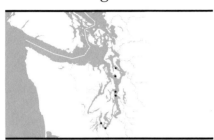

Length 36 cm (14 in)
Wingspread 85 cm (33 in)

**Status and Distribution** The black scoter is an uncommon migrant and winter resident in the Strait of Juan de Fuca and Puget Sound. Midwinter concentrations of 50 to 100 black scoters can be found along Bainbridge Island from Wing to Yeomalt Points (Gardner, 1979). Their numbers are normally scattered, however, with paired and individual black scoters feeding within the larger flocks of surf and white-winged scoters. Useless Bay on Whidbey Island hosts small numbers of wintering black scoters.

**Food and Critical Habitat** This species is much less common than the region's other two scoters, although its food preferences are essentially the same. It dives in shoal waters for molluscs and crustaceans, pries mussels from reefs and ledges, and—like the surf and white-winged scoters—consumes fish spawn.

*Two male common scoters and
a female in Useless Bay*

# Ruddy Duck
*Oxyura jamaicensis*

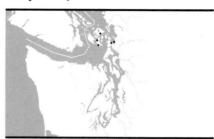

Length 28 cm (11 in)
Wingspread 59 cm (23 in)

**Status and Distribution** The ruddy duck is a winter resident, occurring in scattered flocks in the San Juan Islands, along Hood Canal, and in Puget Sound. At high tide the southwestern edges of Fidalgo Bay are habitually occupied by feeding ruddy ducks. This species frequently forages and rests in protected inlets and small bays such as Barlow Bay on Lopez Island.

**Food and Critical Habitat** Ruddy ducks dive for vegetation, including sedges and algae, as well as small molluscs and crustaceans.

# Hooded Merganser
*Lophodytes cucullatus*

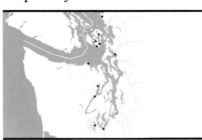

Length 33 cm (13 in)
Wingspread 67 cm (26 in)

**Status and Distribution** An uncommon permanent resident of Washington, this species is occasionally found wintering on saltwater habitats of Puget Sound. The bays and inlets of the San Juan Islands (notable are Mackaye Harbor and Fisherman's Bay on Lopez Island) protected from winter winds and along Hood Canal are frequently feeding locations for this species.

**Food and Critical Habitat** Although these birds prefer fresh water, they occasionally move out to sheltered bays and inlets of Puget Sound to dive in shallow offshore waters for fish and crustaceans.

# Common Merganser
## *Mergus merganser*

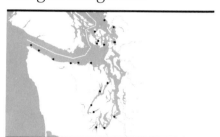

Length 46 cm (18 in)
Wingspread 95 cm (37 in)

# Red-breasted Merganser
## *Mergus serrator*

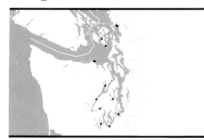

Length 41 cm (16 in)
Wingspread 85 cm (33 in)

**Status and Distribution**  A year-round resident in Washington, common mergansers breed along the lakes and rivers of the interior, move their families out to the estuaries of the Sound by early September, and remain in the vicinity until May. When not on the rivers they are infrequent visitors along the Strait of Juan de Fuca, the San Juan Islands, Hood Canal, and the edges of Puget Sound. Their populations in these locations increase as winter weather freezes the interior waterways. Fall flocks of this species in Dungeness Bay number hundreds of birds.

Fall and winter concentrations of these birds occur in Bellingham and Padilla Bays, and off Tulalip. Commencement Bay still hosts this species, and large winter concentrations occur along the Nisqually Delta and in Budd Inlet of southern Puget Sound (Gardner, 1979).

**Food and Critical Habitat**  Small fish comprise the largest portion of this bird's diet. The merganser is capable of feeding in open-water habitats where tidal currents wash through kelp and over reefs. Immature birds maintain small flocks and frequently can be seen diving for fish above offshore reefs and beds of kelp.

**Status and Distribution**  The red-breasted merganser is a migrant and winter resident from August into May on Puget Sound. Concentrations of more than 100 mergansers have been observed at Dungeness, in Bellingham and Padilla Bays, and in Commencement Bay (Gardner, 1979). Liberty Bay is used by spring flocks of this species.

**Food and Critical Habitat**  In late winter, herring roe represents an important food source for these birds. They gather in pairs and small flocks of eight to ten birds to dive over tideflats and reefs in the offshore waters. They also eat sculpins, sticklebacks, blennies, and occasionally young salmon.

Open bays with relatively protected waters are important to these birds in late winter as they regularly use these areas of calm surfaces for courtship displays. With the gray flanks of the battleship *Missouri* as a backdrop, I once spent several hours in Sinclair Inlet watching the neck-thrusting displays of male mergansers as they competed for females.

*Male red-breasted merganser positions its catch before swallowing*

# Eagles and Hawks
## *Accipitrinae*

The San Juan Islands sustain one of the greatest concentrations of breeding eagles in the world. The food base is sufficient and reasonably free of contaminants, there are plenty of old-growth trees where the birds can roost and construct nests, and the public is admiring and generally concerned for the eagle's welfare. This last portion of the formula is significant as the people of the Northwest have watched with concern the decline of eagle populations throughout the contiguous United States.

There are intangible rewards for maintaining a place for these birds. A glimpse of eagles on the wing sets us momentarily apart from the ordinary and leaves with us a memory of freedom and elegant grace. Such are the images in the San Juan Islands in the fall, when winds strike the heated bluffs, creating geysers of warm air that the raptors soar upon. On the southern flanks of Mt. Erie on Fidalgo Island, Mt. Constitution on Orcas Island, and Mts. Findlayson and Dallas on San Juan Island, eagles rendezvous. The young birds test their inexperienced wings and refine their flight skills. Adult birds assemble to socialize, displayed by short dramatic chases and foot grappling, in which birds lock feet and often tumble hundreds of feet before breaking away only to soar upwards again.

Although golden eagles breed on San Juan Island, only the bald eagle relies on the marine habitat for its livelihood. In the fall, the resident population swells as migrating eagles from the north move into the area to search the waters and beaches for live prey and carrion. When the salmon spawn the birds move to the interior reaches of the Nooksack, Skagit, Sauk, and Stillaguamish Rivers to feed on the carcasses of dead fish.

Marine birds—like any other creatures—spend a great portion of their time looking for their next meal. Nowhere is this activity more noticeable than in the soaring surveys of eagles and hawks. One summer's morning at first light, I awoke to the delicate hum of air passing through and over an eagle's wings. I had placed my sleeping bag on a bluff above a bay facing the Strait of Juan de Fuca. The bird flew across the slope so intent on the beach below that she was oblivious to my presence. She swept back and forth so close to the lip of the cliff I could clearly see her bright yellow toes pressed to the underside of her ice-white tail. The night's tide had apparently delivered nothing of interest, for she never descended and eventually she disappeared around a headland.

On occasion eagles team up to capture a gull or diving bird by taking turns striking at the prey each time it surfaces. Even diving underwater does not provide an avenue of escape for the prey, for if the water is clear the eagles can follow it from above. With good timing one of the two birds is usually prepared to force the quarry into another dive each time it surfaces. Eventually the pursuit ends, when the prey is so exhausted it can no longer dive and is plucked from the water and carried to shore.

The numbers of eagles wintering and breeding in Washington may be the highest total for any of the contiguous states. A 1980 midwinter survey of bald eagles gave a conservative estimate of nearly 1,600 eagles in the state: 935 adults and 663 immature birds (Knight, 1980). A 1981 survey found more than twice as many bald eagles wintering in Washington than in 1980 (Knight, 1981). These numbers are a result of better surveying methods, however, and do not necessarily reflect an increase in actual numbers.

Despite these numbers there is still cause for concern for the bald eagle's welfare over the long term. Habitat loss is the most serious factor contributing to the decline of resident eagles in Washington. Breeding birds require old-growth trees capable of supporting prodigious nests, some of which are over eight-feet wide and over twelve-feet high. Cutting trees with historic nests eliminates an important nesting site and if no other suitable trees are available the birds will not breed.

The Washington State Department of Game currently recommends that a circle of undisturbed habitat 330 feet in diameter is essential around an eyrie throughout the year to preserve the nest site. The Department further recommends that this area be expanded to 660 feet when the birds are breeding.

The food base required by eagles is also diminishing. The problem is most apparent during the winter months when the eagle population is greatest and the birds converge along rivers to feed on the dwindling runs of salmon. A dam once planned for the upper Skagit River would have caused a further decline in native salmon runs. Eagles forced to feed elsewhere because of dam construction would not easily come by new supplies of food, if at all. Competition for other carrion is also keen: in past winters eagles have wandered widely seeking food to scavenge from roadsides, fields, and beaches.

Within the last few years a more obvious impact on Washington's eagle population has come to public attention—the shooting of eagles for their feathers. As recently as 1980, an estimated 75 bald eagles were killed along the delta of the Nooksack. Recent arrests and convictions of suppliers and buyers of eagle feathers will hopefully reduce this lawlessness. Still, there is much work yet to be done to educate people as to the purposes of laws protecting our wildlife and to enforce these laws.

Examination of some of the bodies of eagles killed revealed yet another potential threat to their welfare. Significant amounts of DDT were found in the tissues of two birds. This discovery suggests that we should take a closer look at levels of toxins existing in food webs of the region and examine effects of these poisons on this species.

*Two-year-old bald eagle surveys
the Nisqually Delta*

54

Two adults and an immature bald eagle
at the mouth of the Skagit River

# Bald Eagle
## *Haliaeetus leucocephalus*

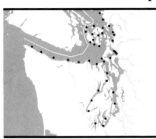

Length 82 cm (32 in)
Wingspread 205 cm (80 in)

**Status and Distribution** A year-round
resident and breeding bird, particularly
along the Strait of Juan de Fuca, in the
San Juan Islands, and in Puget Sound
as well as interior lakes and rivers on
both sides of the Cascades.

In Western Washington, there are
approximately 300 nests; nearly half of
them are active every year (Gardner,
1979). Nash's spring surveys of nesting eagles in the San Juan Islands in
1979 concluded that approximately 42
pairs of eagles were active at nests. Of
these, 35 nests fledged young.

**Food and Critical Habitat** An opportunistic feeder, the bald eagle preys on
a wide range of marine birds—loons,
ducks, gulls, alcids—the young of
breeding birds, and small mammals
from adjacent uplands. Scavenging is
also a typical eagle feeding strategy. It
isn't unusual to see single eagles or
groups of eagles assembled along a
beach near an estuary or on one of the
San Juan Islands in the company of
crows, ravens, and turkey vultures
feeding on the carcass of some animal.

Along the roads of San Juan Island
the rabbits killed by automobiles are an
important part of the diets of resident
bald eagles. A decrease in this food
supply would surely result in a corre-
sponding reduction in the population
of raptors that feed on these rodents.
They could not simply turn to other
food resources, as any possible alterna-
tive resources are likely to be already
exploited by other predators and scavengers.

Isolated old-growth spruce and fir are important to nesting eagles, and snags are essential for resting, cleaning plumage, sunning, and providing suitable vantage points for sighting prey. An eagle soaring is an eagle using energy; perching on top of a towering fir is a more energy-efficient way to spot a meal.

Bald eagles in Puget Sound enjoy considerable popularity, and though this was not always the case, today thousands of people make special efforts to see them, to tally their numbers, and to examine their life histories. In spite of this activity there are still gaps in our knowledge of these birds. While we know that tidal flats and beaches are important foraging grounds for scavenging eagles, we are still unaware to what degree eagles may be building dangerous levels of potentially toxic chemicals in their bodies from eating contaminated carrion. We also do not know what food resources the birds depend on in other locales. Preliminary studies suggest that many "resident" eagles may be very mobile, moving throughout the region and even out of state and back again to favored foraging locations.

*A young marsh hawk*
*pursues a male redwing blackbird*
*near Warm Beach*

# Marsh Hawk
## Circus cyaneus

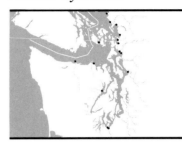

Length 42 cm (16.5 in)
Wingspread 108 cm (42 in)

**Status and Distribution**  Year-round residents of Puget Sound, marsh hawks occasionally breed in fields, hedgerows, and marshes adjacent to salt water. Early records show this species breeding along the outer edges of the Skagit Delta.

The Nooksack, Skagit, and Nisqually River Deltas support several pairs of marsh hawks. The San Juan Islands, with comparatively tiny estuaries and salt marshes, also afford some important habitat for these birds.

**Food and Critical Habitat**  This species patrols the edges of mudflats and diked fields in search of small mice, voles, and moles as well as small birds, reptiles, and insects.

To some extent the same problems potentially affecting eagle populations apply to all raptors. Diminishing food base and lack of suitable breeding locations are often the result of human activity in and around marsh hawk habitat. Draining of wetlands and opening of natural areas to cultivation and development discourages residency of most birds of prey. The degree to which this species is heir to contaminants through its diet is largely unknown, but its hunting habits take it to locations where chemicals are continuously used in agriculture.

# Osprey
## *Pandioninae*

A hunting animal must focus upon its prey with an intensity that may render it oblivious to anything else that exists along the path to its quarry. I once watched a hovering osprey seeking fish with such concentration that it was completely unaware of my presence, even though I was only a few feet away. As I reclined at the edge of the surf in full view, the hunting bird—with legs dangling and wings pumping—studied the water below her. She remained suspended for perhaps ten seconds before moving down the shore to repeat the process.

Eventually the osprey plunged to the water, seized a fish, and flew inland to feed her young. Within the hour she returned to repeat the process, flying close enough that I could see her open and close her powerful toes as if anticipating her next catch.

Ospreys are distinct from other members of the order of diurnal birds of prey because they possess a reversible outer toe. With its flexible feet, exceptionally long talons and toe pads covered with tiny spines, the osprey is ideally equipped for catching and holding slippery fish. On rare occasions the catch proves too great, and the osprey is unable to lift it from the water, or remove its talons from the fish. There are records of drowned ospreys washed ashore with talons still locked in the back of a sturgeon.

This species is long-lived; banded birds have been recaptured more than 20 years after banding. Longevity does not assure survival, however, and ospreys in North America have declined over much of their former range. Pesticides in their diet have affected reproduction in some East Coast ospreys. In the Pacific Northwest, the osprey's population has undoubtedly been affected by the cutting of essential roosting and nesting trees, the encroachment of human settlement, for which it has little tolerance, and the decline of fish populations.

## Osprey
### *Pandion haliaetus*

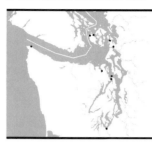

Length 56 cm (22 in)
Wingspread 138 cm (54 in)

**Status and Distribution**  Ospreys are fall and spring migrants and summer residents throughout Washington, including the edges of Puget Sound. They have successfully nested along Rocky and Wescott Bays on San Juan Island, and they can be found feeding along the beaches west of Anacortes and southward to Port Gamble on Hood Canal. A pair has recently attempted nesting at Foulweather Bluff. Farther westward a pair of ospreys from Crocker Lake fish the waters of Discovery Bay (Paulson, 1980), and another pair work Neah Bay for food.

**Food and Critical Habitat**  Feeding almost exclusively on fish, ospreys can be seen patrolling over estuarine waters, off tidal flats, and around the small bays along the Strait of Juan de Fuca. Although food contamination has been implicated in its decline elsewhere, there is insufficient data to suggest that this is the case in Washington.

These raptors have suffered habitat loss from human encroachment near nesting and feeding sites. Their nests are enormous platforms of heavy sticks placed high atop old-growth trees. Ospreys return to these same eyries year after year. Indeed, there is a record of one such eyrie that was used by pairs of ospreys for over 40 years.

# Falcons
## *Falconidae*

I once watched a peregrine hanging in the wind high above the ponds along the outer edge of the Nooksack River. It was November and a storm had pressed the grasses down so that I could look across the flat expanse and see the pintails the falcon was watching. The ducks were safe if they remained on the water close to clumps of cattails where they might retreat if the peregrine attacked: but, either impatient or indifferent to the threat, they took flight. The falcon was moving even before the ducks left the water, accelerating her descent with each pump of her wings. The speed of her flight was unlike any we normally track when watching some animal move under its own power. I was unprepared for it and for a moment she moved out of my field of sight.

The strike sent one pintail rolling in slow motion back to the water and the falcon immediately banked against the wind to turn and retrieve it. This was not to be her meal, however. In the few seconds that it took her to return to her prey a pair of marsh hawks flew in from the edges of the marsh and claimed the duck. The falcon, without protest, circled once then flew southward into the rain.

*A young wintering peregrine feeds along Padilla Bay*

Just as the destiny of many shorebirds, ducks, and alcids is tied to the condition of tidelands, estuaries, and offshore waters, so is the future of the falcon inextricably linked to the presence of its prey. Peregrines, merlins, and occasional gyrfalcons wintering along beaches and estuaries of the Sound are among the most highly evolved of predatory birds. They are sleek-bodied, fast-flying, and stout-legged hunters engaged in a subtle and ceaseless evolutionary race with their prey. Pigeon guillemots, Cassin's and rhinoceros auklets, and tufted puffins all nest in rocky cavities or burrows to avoid these and other avian predators like the large gulls. The crepuscular feeding schedule of some alcids and their habit of flying low over open water are other strategies aimed at avoiding predation.

Conversely, environmental conditions have selected for the falcon's speed and strength in its direct and diving flight. The fast falcon has the edge on the prey if it can gain momentum with a steep dive or a quick ambush. Its accelerated flight requires a clear path to its quarry. A marsh hawk, flying slowly, turns about and hovers in an attempt to snatch a vole from ground cover, whereas the falcon will normally use its speed and strength to overtake a sandpiper or duck and strike it to the ground.

The thousands of dunlin in Padilla and Samish Bays are often pursued by peregrines and merlins. The convoluted flights of these shorebirds are often in response to an approaching predator. On occasion the observer can catch a glimpse of a falcon weaving in and out of the flock like a threadless needle as the fabric of shorebird flight gives way under its advance.

# Gyrfalcon
## *Falco rusticolus*

Length 51 cm (20 in)
Wingspread 123 cm (48 in)

**Status and Distribution**   A casual winter visitor along the northeastern edges of Puget Sound, the gyrfalcon winters more regularly in northeastern Washington. This species was observed in the late 1970s just back from Sandy Point north of Bellingham. The British Columbia tidelands, Fraser River Delta, and lowlands of south Vancouver Island are more often host to this species.

**Food and Critical Habitat**   The gray phase of this large falcon is the one which infrequently ventures into Puget Sound. In Western Washington, the gyrfalcon feeds on ducks and small mammals. Its preference for open habitat takes it to flood plains and estuaries.

*An adult peregrine pursues*
*a pigeon guillemot near Tide Point*
*off Cypress Island*

# Peregrine Falcon
## *Falco peregrinus*

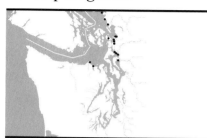

Length 38 cm (15 in)
Wingspread 103 cm (40 in)

**Status and Distribution** An endangered species, the peregrine falcon is primarily seen in Puget Sound as a migrant. While larger numbers of peregrines move through the Strait of Juan de Fuca and Puget Sound on migratory flights, perhaps as many as a dozen birds remain to winter over. Peregrines hunt along the beaches of the San Juan Islands. Arriving as early as October, migrants may remain until March or April.

Samish and Padilla Bays are of critical importance to the welfare of falcons that winter in Washington. They can be found from Point Roberts and Cherry Point southward to the Skagit Delta and Port Susan, and irregularly around Dungeness and Sequim Bays.

A pair of peregrines recently bred in Washington, but whether their numbers are increasing after an historical decline is uncertain. However, because field observations have intensified and improved, the presence of this dramatic bird has been noted with increased frequency.

It is certain that two subspecies of this falcon occur within Puget Sound, the American peregrine and Peale's peregrine falcon. The Peale's is the more marine of the two; its limited population is found along the coasts.

**Food and Critical Habitat** Peregrines are followers of shorebird flocks, ducks, and the alcids that inhabit Puget Sound. Pairs of falcons hunt dunlin and western sandpipers from piling perches in estuaries and mudflats. The peregrines of the Northwest have shown little tolerance for the presence of man and they will normally leave an area actively used by people.

This is a bird that chooses the high, usually inaccessible and undisturbed cliffs for nesting. The few areas of this type that remain within this region are potential breeding locations for peregrines.

# Black Merlin
## *Falco columbarius suckleyi*

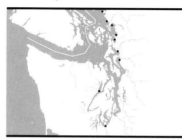

Length 31 cm (12 in)
Wingspread 59 cm (23 in)

**Status and Distribution** The darkest race of this species, the black merlin, is the one most frequently found in Puget Sound. It is a rare resident of Washington, moving south from British Columbia to hunt the tidal flats of Puget Sound from October through March and April.

Merlins passing through or staying in Puget Sound can be seen along most of the major estuaries, particularly the tidal areas along the Nooksack, at Samish and Padilla Bay, Skagit Bay southward to the mouth of the Stillaguamish River, and the Nisqually Flats in southern Puget Sound.

**Food and Critical Habitat** These powerful little falcons are partial to wintering shorebirds, but will feed opportunistically on migratory and resident passerines, including sparrows, juncos, and blackbirds. Insects also are in their diets.

When possible, black merlins perch in trees back from tidal flats. Partially concealed, they launch a pursuit from these locations. Lacking this natural cover, however, these little falcons seem comfortable using the tops of barns or unoccupied vacation homes.

*A black merlin with a Wilson's snipe*

# Rails
## *Rallidae*

Rails are among the most widespread of all families of birds. They've established themselves on most of the continents of the world, and on major and minor islands as well. As a rule they are characterized by their retiring manner and their "thin as a rail" bodies, which allow them to slip silently through the reeds and rushes of the marshes.

An exception to the usual family characteristics is the noisy and gregarious coot, the plump, strong swimming and diving representative of Rallidae found on the salt waters of Puget Sound and the fresh waters of the interior. This species is of the genus Fulica. It has lobate webs on its toes, similar to those of grebes. Unlike grebes, however, coots are adept at walking, and venture well up onto the shore to forage.

Coots as a species are not particularly vulnerable to oiling as most of them remain on fresh water.

## American Coot
*Fulica americana*

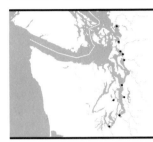

Length 31 cm (12 in)
Wingspread 64 cm (25 in)

**Status and Distribution** The American coot is a locally common migrant and winter resident on Puget Sound. Bellingham and Padilla Bays and the saltwater sloughs at the edges of Fir Island host several hundred wintering coots (Gardner, 1979). Smaller numbers of coots winter along the Edmonds ferry landing, in Shilshole Marina in north Seattle, and at other locations with similar feeding conditions up and down the Sound.

**Food and Critical Habitat** Coots are primarily vegetarians and often gather in estuaries and mudflats to feed.

*Black oystercatchers along the edges of Goose Island in the San Juans*

# Oystercatchers
## *Haematopodidae*

Goose Island sits low in the waters off Cattle Point at the entrance to San Juan Channel. It appears to have been pressed down by heavy-handed winds coming off the Strait of Juan de Fuca. It's a barren spot, with a dearth of cover for terrestrial life. One summer, at slack tide, I swam out to its edges watching bald and golden eagles spiraling up into the clouds on thermals rising from Mt. Finlayson.

I drifted alongside the island occasionally parting the kelp to reveal lurking lingcod and the tiny sculpins and blennies upon which they feed. Visions merged, blurred, and resolved as the waters alternately cleared and clouded with greens and browns of seaweeds, surf grass, and kelp. The pleasures of kinesthesia engulfed me as a swell abruptly carried me off, as casually as the wind propels a gull.

With a heavy rubber hood over my head, it was difficult to hear under water. Sounds came as a surprise. I surfaced to investigate the "piping" calls coming from above. When I poked my head out of the water I discovered I was opposite a rock shelf where a black oystercatcher stretched its head down protesting my presence. Its mate stood directly behind it, and the pair were little more than arm's length away. Without realizing it, I had surfaced opposite a pebble-strewn ledge upon which these birds were nesting. To one side of the parents a fragile youngster was just visible. I took a deep breath through my snorkel and slid from sight, moving down through the kelp and back into deeper water where the island broke away into the channel.

The oystercatcher is characterized by a vertically beveled, bright-colored beak, which is a stout and efficient lever for prying limpets from rocks, probing into mussels, and pummeling small crabs. It is dependent on the intertidal zones throughout the San Juan Islands where it requires isolation for its presence. The orange-red beak and the golden yellow iris of its eyes are a dazzling contrast to its charcoal brown plumage. Its courtship and territorial displays are vivid with demonstrations of mutual bowing, flying chases, and whistle calls.

Because it depends upon food from the intertidal zone and nests in the substrate immediately adjacent to this region, this species would be especially vulnerable to contamination of food and nests resulting from an oil spill.

## Black Oystercatcher
### *Haematopus bachmani*

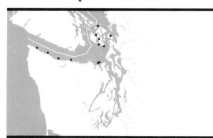

Length 38 cm (15 in)
Wingspread 85 cm (to 33 in)

**Status and Distribution** Black oystercatchers are uncommon permanent residents of the San Juan Islands and suitable rocky locations along the Strait of Juan de Fuca. Their populations have diminished since the 1950s. They are now found regularly only on isolated rocky shores and on small islets.

A survey of the San Juan Archipelago suggests that approximately 41 pairs of oystercatchers are breeding or occupying northern Puget Sound and the San Juan Islands including Goose Island, Low Island, Bare Island, Smith Island, Colville Island, Goose Point, the bays along the south end of Lopez Island, Pointer Island, Long Island, South Peapod Rocks, and Protection Island (Manuwal et al., 1979).

**Food and Critical Habitat** The black oystercatcher feeds almost exclusively on invertebrates of the rocky intertidal zone—particularly limpets, mussels, and chitons. Its beveled beak is ideally suited to handle hard shells. Oysters, contrary to the bird's name, are not a notable percentage of their diet, although they are important to other species of oystercatchers. Hartwick (1973) found that the California mussel (*Mytilus californianus*) and a small crab (*Oedignathus inermis*) were particularly important food for the chicks.

Despite its success in exploiting a habitat that does not attract many competing marine birds, the oystercatcher still suffers from disturbance in feeding and breeding grounds. Nesting (in late May and June) is often disturbed by curious people prowling the rocky shores. Because these are ground-nesting birds they are especially vulnerable to unrestrained pets.

# Plovers
## *Charadriidae*

The far-ranging plovers, with their large, dark eyes, have witnessed places of wild earth, water, and wind that I will never know. I thought of this as I watched a small party of golden plovers flying hundreds of feet above the Strait of Juan de Fuca. They called "Kleee-ee, Kleee-ee," tightened their formation, and plunged into an avalanche of clouds. A long trip northward was still ahead and I wondered if any of them might weaken and fall irretrievably behind. Was there a place in these stout spirits for reflection? Were there moments in these incandescent lives when the faint memory of a comrade might be recalled?

On their migrations to and through this region, the eight-mile arm of Dungeness Spit is a favorite stop-over for plovers. Formed of accreting sediments pulled from the body of the Olympic Peninsula by the surge of the Strait of Juan de Fuca, the Spit cradles assorted ponds and a great bay. In April, under the spring sun that brushes the still pools with shades of pink and lavender, semipalmated and black-bellied plovers join killdeer to feed.

The plover's coloration conceals its presence and finding these birds along the beaches is not always easy. Its light-colored breast blends with the ground color to reduce the starkness of its profile. The bold markings along the face and neck of the killdeer and semipalmated plover tend to "break up" the image of the bird and at a distance it blends miraculously with the blacks, whites, and grays of the feeding grounds. The somber winter plumage of the black-bellied plover is a perfect match for this setting.

Of the plovers visiting greater Puget Sound, the black-bellied and golden are among the most renowned of world travelers. They descend each year from their circumpolar nesting grounds to follow prevailing winds, instinct, and inclination into temperate and tropical habitats. The few golden plovers coming to the Sound are part of a "Pacific" population that breed in western Alaska. They eventually continue southward to Central and South America, or swing southwestward out over the Pacific to winter in Hawaii. Their compact, streamlined bodies are extraordinarily well-suited for conserving the energy needed to travel across great reaches of land and ocean.

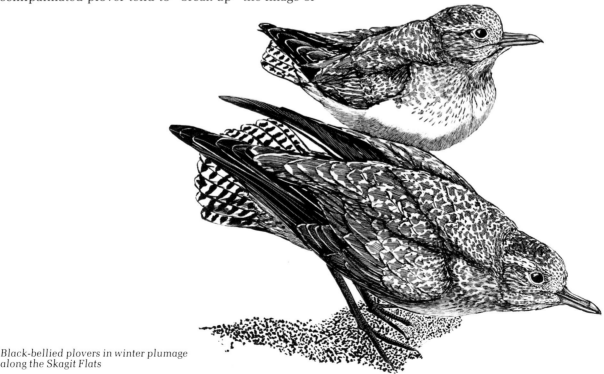

*Black-bellied plovers in winter plumage along the Skagit Flats*

*A pair of killdeers*

# Killdeer
## *Charadrius vociferus*

Length 21 cm (8 in)
Wingspread 51 cm (to 20 in)

**Status and Distribution** The killdeer, one of the most familiar shorebirds, is a year-round resident throughout Puget Sound, along the Strait of Juan de Fuca and into the San Juan Islands.

**Food and Critical Habitat** In marine habitats killdeers consume crustaceans, molluscs, and marine worms. They are active feeders along pebble and sand beaches and mudflats. They nest directly on the substrate, well beyond the water's edge, laying their eggs from the middle of April through the first quarter of June.

During the breeding period, this plover employs an animated distraction display when it senses a threat to its nest. Stepping too close to a killdeer's nest, a human intruder may suddenly find a bent-over, lopsided, wing-dragging bird under foot. Its scratchy pained pipping makes its injured-bird act even more convincing. Predators are tempted to pursue the bird, assuming it to be an easy mark. A sympathetic person might even follow hoping to help. Drawing attention to itself, the killdeer succeeds in diverting potential danger away from its eggs or young.

# Semipalmated Plover
## *Charadrius semipalmatus*

Length 15 cm (6 in)
Wingspread 38 cm (15 in)

**Status and Distribution** Semipalmated plovers are common migrants in May and from July to late September along the Strait of Juan de Fuca and on Puget Sound. These birds, like most others of their family utilize the beaches of the outer coast, Strait of Juan de Fuca, and Puget Sound as an essential stopover between nesting grounds along the Arctic Coast and wintering areas farther south. Dungeness Spit and San Juan Island's southern beaches are important to this species.

**Food and Critical Habitat** These boldly marked little plovers scurry over sandy beaches and mudflats picking up marine worms, molluscs, and crustaceans. In the spring they are common at Dungeness Spit, where estuarine conditions and protected beaches host abundant organisms upon which to feed.

*A semipalmated plover*

# Black-bellied Plover
*Pluvialis squatarola*

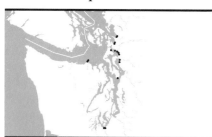

Length 24 cm (9.5 in)
Wingspread 59 cm (23 in)

# American Golden Plover
*Pluvialis dominica*

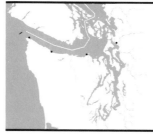

Length 23 cm (9 in)
Wingspread 56 cm (22 in)

**Status and Distribution** These birds are common spring and fall migrants and less common winter residents on the Strait of Juan de Fuca and within Puget Sound and the San Juan Islands. The spring flights of the black-bellied plovers bring them through the region in April and May heading north. They begin to return from their arctic nesting grounds as early as July and continue into November (Gardner, 1979).

The shores along the mouths of the Nisqually, Stillaguamish, and Skagit Rivers are utilized by hundreds of these birds. Samish and Padilla Bays are also important feeding locations. Along Whidbey Island black-bellied plovers frequent Cultus and Dugualla Bays. Farther west, Dungeness Spit and Bay host hundreds of plovers.

**Food and Critical Habitat** In marine habitats these birds consume worms, small molluscs, and insects along mud-flats and beaches. Protected shores along estuaries are especially favored, as well as nearby agricultural fields.

*Black-bellied plovers in breeding plumage near Penn Cove*

**Status and Distribution** A rare spring and uncommon fall migrant, the golden plover utilizes the Washington coast and Puget Sound during its remarkable 18,000-mile journey to and from the Southern Hemisphere. Golden plovers migrating through Washington from the Arctic may be headed either to Argentina or Tahiti depending on the origins of their breeding population (Paulson, 1980). Dungeness Bay and the smaller protected bays westward along the Strait of Juan de Fuca occasionally host this species.

**Food and Critical Habitat** The diet of the golden plover is similar to that of the black-bellied plover. Both species consume worms, small molluscs, and insects from mudflats and fine sand beaches. Both also move to agricultural fields just inland from marine shores to feed.

# Sandpipers
## *Scolopacidae*

Along the tideflats beyond Hat Slough, a vaporous ribbon of sandpipers stretches out for nearly a mile. These are dunlin, thousands of them forming a huge flock that tapers, then swells, as other birds join the relentless movement of the line. When they turn, the flock suddenly compresses and reverses itself in a soundless explosion of light as their white breasts are caught in the sun's glow.

I wonder what compels these birds to move forward through frosty air and then wheel back along the iced edges of the slough. What leads them? What subtle cue causes the flock to turn with such synchrony, and then signals them so suddenly to a halt that they settle over the shore like a diaphanous veil? Part of the pleasure of watching such a spectacle is knowing that there are no simple explanations and one can simply enjoy being set adrift in fantasies of flight.

On the ground, sandpipers are not nearly so easy to see. Their heads and backs are cryptically colored and their light undersides pick up ground color, reducing contrast with their surroundings. At a distance, winter tidal flats can appear barren, but a closer look finds sandpipers probing into the soft mud.

Sandpipers come in assorted sizes, with varying lengths of legs and bills that permit the different members of this family to exploit feeding niches both above and below the water's edge. The small- and medium-sized sandpipers occasionally compete for the same food. Least and western sandpipers and dunlin prefer the beach itself; the dunlin probe deeply while the two smaller sandpipers poke the substrate and snatch surface food. The fleet-footed sanderling feeds at the edge of the surf, racing back and forth before its onslaught. Dowitchers regularly wade chest-deep in shallows where they feed with their sensitive tubular bills for underwater animals.

Surfbirds, tattlers, and rock sandpipers are the solitary members of this family. They feed along the raw edges of rocky shores where water incessantly batters the land. Stout-bodied and thick-footed, they are ably suited to bob and trot about in this tumultuous environment. Turnstones occasionally feed here as well, but they also occupy the coarse gravel beaches where they can pry and poke about for small crustaceans with their stout bills.

The large sandpipers prey on creatures that are too large for the smaller species to handle. The scythe-billed whimbrel strolls at the tide's edge looking for mudshrimp burrows. When it spots a burrow it inserts its bill and probes along the passageway until it finds the shrimp. It then seizes its prey, and with a twist of its long neck, extracts its meal.

The stilt-legged greater yellowlegs wades through waters up to its abdomen—weight forward, leaning well out over the water—scouting for small fish.

Like other families of birds in Puget Sound this group has numerous members that rely on the food resources of the area's estuaries. The Nisqually, Skagit, and Nooksack river estuaries support sizeable populations of these birds. As agricultural and industrial activity intensifies, however, toxic by-products and wastes moving into the estuarine food web will, over time, have significant impact on these aggregations of birds. One need only compare the highly developed Puyallup River estuary, noting the relative absence of shorebirds, to realize the effect of industrialization on the feeding grounds of these species.

Other threats to shorebird feeding habitat are dredging of tidal flats, the presence of log booms, and water pollution. As a rule, however, shorebird feeding, flocking, and roosting habits preclude direct contact with oil. A more immediate disruption to shorebirds, however, is human intrusion in their feeding habitat. As the edges of bay beaches become fringed with summer cabins, there are more people and pets strolling along the water's edge at low tide who unknowingly discourage shorebirds from feeding at critical times.

Remote and undisturbed beaches and tidelands are the critical primary feeding areas. Here, too, courtship and pair bonding can occur in late winter and early spring.

*From top: Least sandpipers, sanderlings (in breeding plumage) and dunlin feed in spring at Cultus Bay*

66

# Surfbird
*Aphriza virgata*

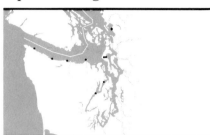

Length 21 cm (8 in)
Wingspread 46 cm (18 in)

**Status and Distribution**  This species occurs widely but in scattered numbers from July to May along Hood Canal, the Strait of Juan de Fuca, and the San Juan Islands. In the early 1900s, surfbirds were not uncommon at Seattle beaches and along Dungeness Spit (Jewett et al., 1953). Today, however, they have retreated to the smaller, more isolated islands of the San Juans. Penn Cove at Whidbey Island also regularly hosts surfbirds, and Chuckanut Island hosts 70 birds.

**Food and Critical Habitat**  Like the black oystercatcher, these robust little birds forage at the sea's turbulent edges. The species' name *Aphriza*, of Greek derivation, is well chosen, for it means in essence "I live in the sea foam."

Surfbirds are particularly fond of small mussels, up to a quarter of an inch long. They also feed on other molluscs and crustaceans in the rocky intertidal zone and on occasion, along coarse gravel beaches.

*Surfbird along the Strait of Juan de Fuca*

# Ruddy Turnstone
*Arenaria interpres*

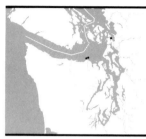

Length 18 cm (7 in)
Wingspread 46 cm (to 18 in)

**Status and Distribution**  Although the ruddy turnstone is an abundant spring migrant along Washington's coast, it is uncommon in spring and fall migrations along the Strait of Juan de Fuca, the San Juan Islands, and Puget Sound. In the mid-1970s, modest numbers of ruddy turnstones were observed in May (20 birds) and June (60 birds) at Dungeness Spit, and in February (25 birds) farther east at March Point (Mathematical Sciences Northwest, 1977).

**Food and Critical Habitat**  Versatile feeders, these birds consume marine worms, crustaceans, small molluscs, and insects. They forage along sandy beaches, over mudflats, along salt marshes, and on rocky shores and jetties (Gardner, 1979).

# Black Turnstone
*Arenaria melanocephala*

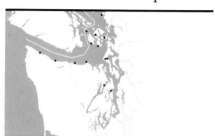

Length 18 cm (7 in)
Wingspread 46 cm (to 18 in)

**Status and Distribution** Black turnstones are regular migrants in the spring from April into May and in the fall, appearing as early as July and staying through October. They occur along the Strait of Juan de Fuca, in the San Juan Islands, and on Hood Canal and South Puget Sound.

This species is also a less common winter resident in the northern reaches of this region. The gravel and cobble beaches of Mackaye Harbor on Lopez Island regularly host wintering turnstones. Flocks of this species wander widely through the San Juans and onto numerous islets and exposed reefs to feed. A mid-1970s count showed Penn Cove on Whidbey Island hosting 225 of these birds in April and Deer Lagoon hosting 150 in September (Mathematical Sciences Northwest, 1977).

**Food and Critical Habitat** Black turnstones scurry and poke over rocky beaches, headlands, and offshore rocks searching for limpets, barnacles, and assorted small crustaceans. Their stout bills are effective in dislodging food from rocky niches and reaching the undersides of rocks where marine animals have retreated or attached themselves.

*Black turnstones take to flight*

# Common Snipe
*Gallinago gallinago*

Length 23 cm (9 in)
Wingspread 38 cm (to 15 in)

**Status and Distribution** Although it prefers freshwater habitats, the snipe is frequently found as a fall and spring migrant and winter resident along Puget Sound, and is occasionally seen feeding in salt marshes along the Strait of Juan de Fuca, in the San Juan Islands, and on Hood Canal. In early winter, the northern edges of Fir Island are used by snipe.

**Food and Critical Habitat** When freshwater marshes are frozen in winter, the snipe moves to salt marshes to feed on marine worms and small crustaceans.

# Spotted Sandpiper
*Actitis macularia*

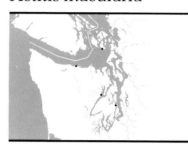

Length 16 cm (6.25 in)
Wingspread 35 cm (13.5 in)

**Status and Distribution** The spotted sandpiper is an uncommon migrant and rare winter resident along Puget Sound, Hood Canal, the Strait of Juan de Fuca, and protected bays and inlets within the San Juan Islands.

**Food and Critical Habitat** This species forages for small crustaceans and marine worms in fine sand and mud beaches along estuaries. Within protected bays with pebble beaches, sandpipers probe for animals in the substrate and surf-strewn seaweed.

# Whimbrel
## Numenius phaeopus

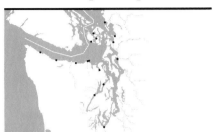

Length 36 cm (14 in)
Wingspread 82 cm (to 32 in)

**Status and Distribution** A common spring and fall migrant in Puget Sound, the whimbrel occasionally winters here. Solitary birds and pairs are not uncommon in the San Juan Islands, and along the Strait of Juan de Fuca and Hood Canal. Dungeness Bay is of particular importance to these birds.

**Food and Critical Habitat** Whimbrels forage along the edge of the tide on mudflats for mudshrimp. Crabs and worms are also common prey of the whimbrel on the mudflats, back bays, saltwater sloughs, and marshes of the region. Harbor edges are popular feeding places.

# Wandering Tattler
## Heteroscelus incanus

Length 22 cm (8.75 in)
Wingspread 49 cm (to 19 in)

**Status and Distribution** Found principally on the coast and the open beaches of the Strait of Juan de Fuca, wandering tattlers are common spring migrants from mid-April to late May. They return from their breeding grounds to migrate through this region from July into October. Recently, tattlers have been sighted along the rocky breakwaters at Shilshole Bay.

**Food and Critical Habitat** The tattler seeks small molluscs, marine worms, and crustaceans along rocky and coarse gravel beaches.

# Dunlin
## Calidris alpina

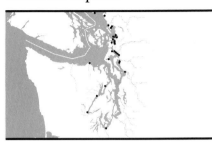

Length 18 cm (7 in)
Wingspread 38 cm (to 15 in)

**Status and Distribution** A common migrant and winter resident on Puget Sound from October to early May, flocks of dunlin in the tens of thousands can be found on Skagit, Padilla, and Samish Bays. Smaller concentrations are seen along Hood Canal, at Nisqually Delta, and Discovery, Sequim, and Dungeness Bays. Along Whidbey Island, Cultus and Dugualla Bays are important to dunlin, as are Warm Beach and Fidalgo Bay.

**Food and Critical Habitat** It is typically the great flocks of dunlin that trace fluid silhouettes over the stark winter backdrop of frozen mudflats and frosted islands in Puget Sound. As the tide changes, the birds move along its edge probing soft substrate for amphipods, insects, worms, and small molluscs.

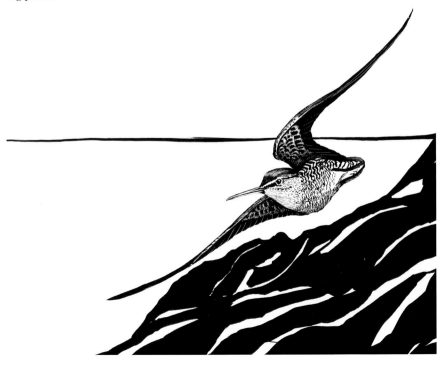

*Wandering tattler*

*A flock of dunlin in winter plumage over Samish Bay*

# Western Willet
## *Catoptrophorus semipalmatus*

Length 35 cm (13.5 in)
Wingspread 69 cm (to 27 in)

**Status and Distribution**   The willet is a very rare fall migrant along Washington's outer coast, the northwestern portions of Puget Sound, and the Straits of Georgia and Juan de Fuca. Some earlier records find the birds occurring along Dungeness Spit, in Whatcom County, and as far south as Seattle and Tacoma (Jewett et al., 1953).

**Food and Critical Habitat**   These birds favor bays with mudflats and mixed fine sand beaches where they can probe for marine worms, small crabs, and insects.

# Greater Yellowlegs
## *Tringa melanoleuca*

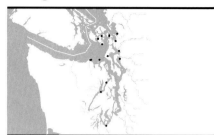

Length 28 cm (11 in)
Wingspread 64 cm (to 25 in)

**Status and Distribution**   Greater yellowlegs are common spring migrants from April through May, and in the late summer-to-fall migration from early July through October. A few yellowlegs winter in Puget Sound around the shallow leeward waters of inlets and bays in the San Juan Islands. Dungeness Bay and Hood Canal also host migrating and wintering yellowlegs. On Cypress Island, a two-mile stretch of coast between Strawberry Bay and Tide Point provided suitable foraging habitat for over 100 yellowlegs in a mid-1970s count (Mathematical Sciences Northwest, 1977).

**Food and Critical Habitat**   These stately birds wade the margins of bays and shallow waters to stab and snap up small fish, mussels, and crabs.

# Lesser Yellowlegs
## *Tringa flavipes*

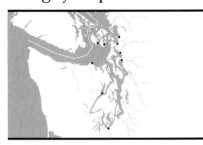

Length 22 cm (8.75 in)
Wingspread 51 cm (to 20 in)

**Status and Distribution**   An uncommon spring and common fall migrant on Puget Sound, the lesser yellowlegs may be found from April through May and from July into October.

**Food and Critical Habitat**   These miniatures of their larger namesakes wade and occasionally swim along the margins of sand and pebble beaches, daintily probing the waters for tiny shellfish and marine worms.

# Red Knot
## *Calidris canutus*

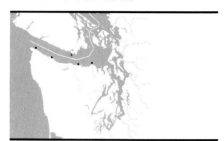

Length 23 cm (9 in)
Wingspread 51 cm (20 in)

**Status and Distribution** A rare migrant in Puget Sound during the spring and fall, the greatest concentrations of this species occur on Washington's outer coast. They are most likely to be seen in Puget Sound during the fall (Paulson, 1980). Washington's coast is an important refueling location for this species as they make their way north to their nesting grounds above the Arctic Circle.

**Food and Critical Habitat** Knots feed on small molluscs and crustaceans found in sand and pebble beaches and in the fine sediment of salt marshes and estuaries.

# Pectoral Sandpiper
## *Calidris melanotos*

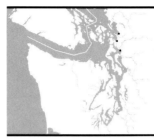

Length 19 cm (7.5 in)
Wingspread 44 cm (to 17 in)

**Status and Distribution** The pectoral sandpiper is a fairly common fall migrant throughout Puget Sound from September to early November. It is a rare spring migrant during April and May.

**Food and Critical Habitat** This species is most likely to be found in salt marsh habitats feeding on crustaceans and insects. Their striped and mottled brown backs render them all but invisible as they feed within the grassy ground cover of the marshes.

*Two pectoral sandpipers*

### Short-billed Dowitcher
*Limnodromus griseus*

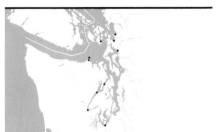

Length 24 cm (9.5 in)
Wingspread 49 cm (to 19 in)

**Status and Distribution** Short-billed dowitchers are common migrants from early August to December and from mid March to May. They occur in northern and southern Puget Sound and occasionally in salt marshes of the San Juan Islands. Hood Canal also provides feeding habitat for short-billed dowitchers. Dungeness Bay and Spit are important feeding areas for late spring and early fall flocks of this species.

**Food and Critical Habitat** This species prefers to feed in saltwater sloughs and estuaries, probing the mud and fine sand for marine worms, crustaceans, and molluscs.

*Short-billed dowitchers feeding off Nisqually Delta*

### Long-billed Dowitcher
*Limnodromus scolopaceus*

Length 26 cm (10 in)
Wingspread 49 cm (to 19 in)

**Status and Distribution** Along northern and southern Puget Sound, this species is a common migrant from the middle of April to May and again from August into October. This species uses salt marsh areas in the San Juan Islands, and in the fall is seen at Padilla and Skagit Bays and McAllister Creek in the Nisqually Delta.

**Food and Critical Habitat** Like the short-billed dowitcher, the long-billed probes mudflats, fine sediment beaches, and estuarine shores for marine worms, small molluscs, and crustaceans (Gardner, 1979). Unlike the short-billed, this dowitcher is common in freshwater habitats as well.

### Western Sandpiper
*Calidris mauri*

Length 13 cm (5.25 in)
Wingspread 36 cm (to 14 in)

**Status and Distribution** Along with the dunlin, this is probably the most abundant shorebird in Washington (Gardner, 1979). It is a migrant, occurring from late March to May and from the end of June to early November.

Although the greatest concentrations of western sandpipers appear on Washington's outer coasts, Dungeness, Skagit, Padilla, Samish, and Fidalgo Bays south to the Nisqually Delta also host thousands of these birds during their spring and fall migrations (Gardner, 1979).

**Food and Critical Habitat** These birds are dependent upon beaches adjacent to estuaries and tidal flats where the mud and fine sand sediment supplies amphipods and marine worms.

Sandy spits attract this species as roosting sites. They are also fond of roosting in concentrated clusters on log booms and exposed flanks of beached snags where a partial moat of water assures some protection from terrestrial predators.

# Semipalmated Sandpiper
## *Calidris pusilla*

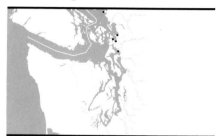

Length 13 cm (5 in)
Wingspread 31 cm (to 12 in)

**Status and Distribution** Migrating up and down the continent principally east of the Rocky Mountains, these sandpipers occur only peripherally in the Puget Sound region in the fall and spring. Washington's earliest record of this species in Puget Sound was on Fidalgo Island in 1858 (Jewett et al., 1953). Since that time there have been reports of the bird occurring at times with western sandpipers, from Blaine southward. When examining flocks of western and least sandpipers, one should look carefully for the presence of the rare and often difficult to identify semipalmated sandpiper.

**Food and Critical Habitat** This bird, among the smallest of the sandpipers, feeds on small molluscs, crustaceans, insects, and worms (Bent, 1927). Like western and least sandpipers, these birds favor mudflats adjacent to estuaries with their substrate of fine sediment.

# Least Sandpiper
## *Calidris minutilla*

Length 12 cm (4.75 in)
Wingspread 29 cm (to 11.5 in)

**Status and Distribution** The least sandpiper is a common migrant from late March into May, and from July into October. It occurs less commonly as a winter resident. Hundreds of these birds have been observed on the beaches along Dungeness Spit, Skagit Flats, and Sinclair Inlet. The mudflats of the Nisqually Delta are important to late winter and early spring flocks of this species. Cultus Bay on Whidbey Island has historically been good habitat for least sandpipers and the eastern edges of Fidalgo Bay are also important.

**Food and Critical Habitat** This tiny sandpiper utilizes the coasts and inland beaches of the Strait of Juan de Fuca and Puget Sound as a critical waystation during migration. While in this area, least sandpipers feed on amphipods and worms from mud and fine sand beaches. Elevated mudflats are used at high tide.

# Marbled Godwit
## *Limosa fedoa*

Length 41 cm (16 in)
Wingspread 82 cm (to 32 in)

**Status and Distribution** The marbled godwit is a rare spring migrant that has diminished greatly from the former numbers on the Washington Coast. Early in the 20th century it occurred along the Tacoma tideflats.

**Food and Critical Habitat** A deep prober, this species seeks small molluscs and crustaceans in the beaches of fine sand and mud adjacent to bays and estuaries.

74

## Sanderling
*Calidris alba*

Length 17 cm (6.5 in)
Wingspread 38 cm (to 15 in)

**Status and Distribution** This species
is a common migrant in the spring from
March through May, and fall from September into November. Small flocks of
sanderlings winter along the Strait of
Juan de Fuca, in the San Juan Islands,
Hood Canal, and in northern and southern Puget Sound. Of some importance
are Cultus Bay on Whidbey Island, Dabob Bay on Hood Canal and Dungeness
Spit. The numbers of sanderlings present in the region appeared to increase
in the 1970s.

**Food and Critical Habitat** Couch
(1966) found that sanderlings, feeding
in the company of other shorebirds on
Puget Sound, consume amphipods, marine worms, and small fish. Sandy
beaches and the edge of the surf are preferred feeding locations.

## Long-billed Curlew
*Numenius americanus*

Length 49 cm (19 in)
Wingspread 97 cm (to 38 in)

**Status and Distribution** Rare spring
and fall migrants along the Strait of
Juan de Fuca and in Puget Sound, these
birds are widespread in eastern Washington during breeding season. A loss
of nesting habitat to cultivation has
forced a decline in this species in
Washington.

**Food and Critical Habitat** The cur-
lews' migrations bring them to salt
marshes, tideflats, and estuarine shallows along Puget Sound where they
consume molluscs, crustaceans, and
worms. Their extraordinarily long bills
permit them to probe deep into the burrows of their prey.

*Rock sandpiper*

# Rock Sandpiper
## *Calidris ptilocnemis*

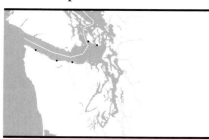

Length 21 cm (8 in)
Wingspread 38 cm (to 15 in)

**Status and Distribution**    Uncommon visitors during winter along the Strait of Juan de Fuca and northern Puget Sound, rock sandpipers are much more abundant on Washington's outer coast (Paulson, 1980).

**Food and Critical Habitat**    This robust, short-legged sandpiper works the rocky shores, jetties, and exposed reefs of Puget Sound for crustaceans and molluscs. It is sometimes found in the company of surfbirds and black turnstones, which also exploit the winter food resources of these locations.

# Sharp-tailed Sandpiper
## *Calidris acuminata*

Length 18 cm (7 in)
Wingspread 44 cm (17 in)

**Status and Distribution**    This sandpiper is a late August through November migrant. It moves along the Washington coast and into Puget Sound, sometimes in the company of pectoral sandpipers (Gardner, 1979).

**Food and Critical Habitat**    Like other sandpipers, the sharp-tailed favors crustaceans, molluscs, and insects when feeding in the marine habitat. Salt marshes rich in flowering Salicornia and grassy edges of mixed fine and sandy beaches are favorite habitats of these birds.

# Baird's Sandpiper
## *Calidris bairdii*

Length 15 cm (6 in)
Wingspread 41 cm (to 16 in)

**Status and Distribution**    These birds are uncommon fall migrants on Puget Sound. From July through September they stop here briefly as they travel from arctic nesting grounds to points as far south as Argentina and Chile for the winter. They are very rare in spring, occurring if at all from late April through May, and are not seen most years.

**Food and Critical Habitat**    These sandpipers eat insects and their larvae, feeding along grassy shores at the margins of beaches.

*Foraging sharp-tailed sandpiper*

# Phalaropes
## *Phalaropodinae*

Moving down Haro Strait one July afternoon, Ken Balcomb and I approached San Juan Channel in his small boat. We reflected over a memorable afternoon spent observing the feeding activity of the orcas of "J" Pod as they moved along the southwest end of San Juan Island. Several of these formidable mammals had approached us, swimming parallel to our boat with the "conning tower" dorsal fin of the big males little more than an arm's length away. Their periodic dives left dimples ten and fifteen feet in diameter at the water's surface.

Our craft bounced and careened along in the chop as the orcas moved smoothly below, far better fitted to the turbulent water than we were. Swells higher than our boat came in from the south over Salmon Banks and clashed with the currents pouring into the strait between San Juan and Lopez Islands. Suddenly, looking into this turmoil and feeling more than a little awed by it, I was surprised to glimpse a flock of what first appeared to be sandpipers. Their flight path snaked below and around the crests of the swells and into the troughs of waves.

We lost sight of them momentarily as they cleared a descending wall of water. When the swell had subsided, the little flock could be seen swimming frantically along the face of a following wave. These were northern phalaropes, and though from a distance they may appear to be typical shorebirds by size and their twisted and hurried flight, their ability to feed at the surface of deep waters distinguishes them from the other families.

The northern phalarope is the species most likely to be seen here: the red and Wilson's phalaropes are seen only occasionally within the region. All species are characterized by lobate toes that enable them to operate effectively both wading and swimming. Their broad bodies and dense plumage further suit them to a largely aquatic—if not pelagic—life. When feeding from the water's surface, these birds—whether in groups or individually—whirl about and stir the water with their feet, a strategy that apparently sweeps food closer to the surface where they can easily seize it.

Phalaropes are also characterized by a reversal of roles in courtship and brood rearing. The female is larger and more ornately colored than the male, and it is she who initiates the courtship ritual leading to copulation. The drab male constructs the nest, incubates the eggs, and guards the young.

There is little information on the effects of oil spills on phalaropes, but given their surface feeding habits, one can assume that bilge oil or tank cleanings dumped in offshore waters represent a potential threat of contamination of food and plumage.

*Northern phalaropes feeding in Haro Strait*

# Red Phalarope
## *Phalaropus fulicaria*

Length 19 cm (7.5 in)
Wingspread 38 cm (15 in)

**Status and Distribution** A spring and fall migrant from August through November, the red phalarope occurs along the Washington coast and occasionally forages in the outer edges of the Strait of Juan de Fuca. Early records found these birds well into Puget Sound as far south as Tacoma and Steilacoom (Jewett et al., 1953).

**Food and Critical Habitat** When not breeding, these are open-water birds that forage off the outer coast and are the most pelagic of the three phalaropes. At sea, phalaropes are referred to as "whale birds." Their circling flocks were clues to sailors to the whereabouts of whales. When the birds see "blow" spouts they fly toward them and feed on parasites from the whales' backs or on bits of uneaten krill left in the water. They also eat tiny fish.

*A pair of Wilson's phalaropes— female (left), male (right)*

# Northern Phalarope
## *Phalaropus lobatus*

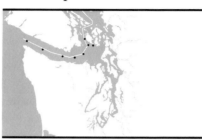

Length 15 cm (6 in)
Wingspread 36 cm (14 in)

**Status and Distribution** Northern phalaropes are uncommon migrants from late April through May and common migrants from early July to October in Puget Sound. Greatest concentrations of this species occur along the Strait of Juan de Fuca where nonbreeding birds occasionally remain through the summer. Haro Strait and the larger inter-island passages attract flocks of migrating northern phalaropes.

**Food and Critical Habitat** Gathering in flocks of sometimes hundreds of birds, this species frequents tidal rips where small plankton-feeding fish and invertebrates, particularly krill, feed. This phalarope is partial to locations where the waters of entrance channels converge with inside waters. The clashing waters stir sediments and accumulated organic debris, which attracts feeding animals that are food for the foraging birds.

# Wilson's Phalarope
## *Phalaropus tricolor*

Length 19 cm (7.5 in)
Wingspread 41 cm (16 in)

**Status and Distribution** This species is a rare migrant in March and April and from July through November. In Puget Sound this species breeds east of the Cascades in Washington. There are records of Wilson's phalaropes breeding on the Tacoma tideflats in the late 1930s (Jewett et al., 1953). Whether Western Washington still has suitable breeding habitat for these strikingly beautiful birds is in doubt, although there was a possible nesting noted near Keystone on Whidbey Island in the mid 1970s (Mathematical Sciences Northwest, 1977).

**Food and Critical Habitat** When visiting Puget Sound this species consumes insects and insect larvae in shallow waters of salt marshes and over beaches of mud and fine sand.

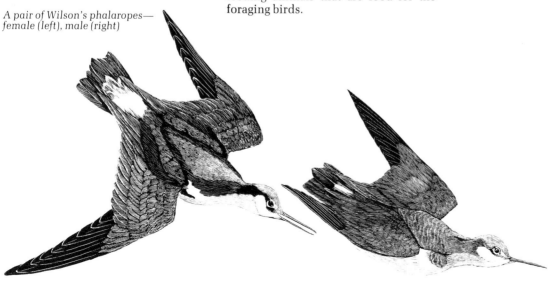

# Jaegers
## *Stercorariinae*

Bonaparte's gulls, flying shoreward from where they have been dipping for fish, are a bright contrast to the somber September waters bordering Whidbey Island. Most adults have lost their black hoods, and at a distance it's difficult to distinguish them from the young birds that were hatched earlier in the year. As they approach the island a dark form pitches into their midst, singles out a young gull and—beak to tail—relentlessly pursues it. The desperate gull disgorges its fish, and its pursuer, a parasitic jaeger, breaks away to snatch it in midair. With a quick flipping turn the jaeger is locked into the chase of yet another gull.

The name jaeger is derived from the German *jager*, meaning hunter. Although these birds do hunt effectively, we have projected our own sense of values upon the species and often refer to them as pirates when they seek to take the catches of other birds.

The wings, tail, and body of the jaeger is ideally formed for a bird of prey. The wing is tapered like a tern's, but the primary feathers have shafts similar in strength to those of a falcon. This enables the jaeger to make abrupt turns, accelerate, and dive rapidly. Long central tail feathers work like a rudder as the jaeger makes quick aerobatic turns when pursuing other birds. Its feet are webbed for paddling and equipped with sharp toenails to hold prey that it tears with a stout hooked beak.

Jaegers nest circumpolarly on arctic tundra in the summer, then wander southward over marine waters—and on rare occasions inland—in the winter.

*Parasitic jaeger pirates catch of
young Bonaparte's gull off Whidbey Island*

# Long-tailed Jaeger
*Stercorarius longicaudus*

Length 46 cm (18 in)

**Status and Distribution** A very rare fall migrant, the long-tailed jaeger arrives with parasitic jaegers as early as September to pass through the San Juan Islands, the Strait of Juan de Fuca, and Puget Sound to southern waters for the winter. It is not seen here every year as most migrating jaegers stay off Washington's coast. There were sightings of these birds in 1980 off northeastern Lopez Island (Orians, 1980).

**Food and Critical Habitat** A capable pirate, the jaeger obtains its food by stealing the catches of gulls and terns.

# Pomarine Jaeger
*Stercorarius pomarinus*

Length 44 cm (17 in)
Wingspread 123 cm (48 in)

**Status and Distribution** Rare fall migrants in the outer Strait of Juan de Fuca and in Puget Sound, these jaegers are more common off Washington's coast. They occur in April and May and from August into October (Manuwal et al., 1979).

**Food and Critical Habitat** Whether off the coast or within the Strait, the pomarine jaeger is a capable fishing bird and predator, taking food from medium-sized gulls and terns. On open waters they like to scavenge as well, eating refuse from boats or scraps from meals of other marine animals.

# Parasitic Jaeger
*Stercorcarius parasiticus*

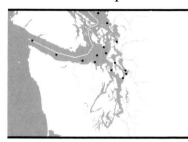

Length 41 cm (16 in)

**Status and Distribution** Parasitic jaegers are rare visitors from April through May, but are fairly common migrants from late July through December in the Strait of Juan de Fuca and Puget Sound. Saratoga Passage and the waters off Everett have historically hosted jaegers.

**Food and Critical Habitat** These birds favor open waters, particularly along the open coast. They are also found along channels and reefs of the interior of Puget Sound and in the large estuaries. Open waters of major entrance channels are of particular importance (Gardner, 1979).

A major source of sustenance for these birds is food obtained by forcing gulls and terns to disgorge their meals. They also feed on edible refuse. When the Everett sanitary landfill was operating, migrating parasitic jaegers habitually waylaid gulls flying out brim full of the city's best garbage.

# Gulls and Terns
## *Laridae*

Flat and elongated, Colville Island sits off Lopez Island's southeastern reaches appearing barren and lifeless in winter. Its surface, sculpted by harsh southerly winds, begins to brighten in late March with a mantle of early spring grasses. By the end of April and into early fall, this site is a tumult as thousands of glaucous-winged gulls vie for territories to brood eggs and feed young. Their din can be heard miles away and the bright white of their collective plumage settles like fresh snow over Colville's rocky top.

This island is a sanctuary for marine birds; by law humans are prohibited from entering without special permission. Such restrictions, however, do not apply to foraging eagles. When the powerful silhouette of this hunter sets a course for the breeding grounds, there is a frantic eruption of protest and distress calls. As the predator approaches, a canopy of incessantly crying birds appears above the island.

Over several years I've observed this drama with little variation. The eagles, rearing young in eyries on Lopez and San Juan Islands, normally hunt at dawn. As the gulls take to the air the hunter veers to one side, drops across the edge of the cloud of birds, and disappears on the island's surface. It reappears a few minutes later, its wings flapping heavily, and heads back across the channel to Lopez, a few gulls chasing it half-heartedly. Clutched to the eagle's body is a young, lifeless gull. I have never witnessed an eagle capture a live gull. Most of the prey taken from the gull's breeding grounds are probably already dead, or close to death. Life in the gull colony is fiercely competitive, and the eagle is quick to retrieve the bodies of those that fail to survive.

The gulls of Puget Sound are the most familiar of marine birds. When most people think of beaches and salt water the seagull is part of the image. The term "seagull," however, is misleading, for many members of this family are found far inland, where they feed and breed. Most gulls that do favor saltwater habitat are normally found close to the shore and in this region only the black-legged kittiwake habitually ventures beyond the sight of land to become a genuine "seagull."

The larger members of this family are bold and aggressive, and though breeding habitat has diminished for some gulls, they have found plenty to eat in the presence of humankind. Some follow tractors in the fields, seeking insects and small mammals exposed by the process of cultivation. Others beg handouts from ferry passengers, clean up after picnickers, or seize marine animals exposed by clam diggers. The most common gull of the region, the glaucous-winged, habitually feeds on garbage at landfill sites. It also joins other gulls over schools of herring driven close to the surface by feeding salmon, rhinoceros auklets, puffins, or murres. The raft of feeding birds is a mob of flapping wings, plunging bodies, and raucous voices bickering and vying for prey.

Gulls are big enough to be easily seen and have interesting habits, so it's not surprising that people study them. They have a remarkable and varied repertoire of calls, postures, and displays to sound alarms, rally other gulls, frighten rivals, stimulate mates, or attract the attention of youngsters.

There are pronounced physical differences between gulls and terns. Gulls generally have a sturdier build and possess a heavier, slightly hooked bill. They have webbed toes and stout legs, well positioned both for swimming and ambling over land. The pointed-winged, fork-tailed terns, on the other hand, are built to remain aloft and are weak swimmers. When they see a fish or shrimp they momentarily hover or circle back, then plunge headfirst into the water where they seize prey with their sharp slender bill.

All gulls and terns wander and most migrate to and from breeding and wintering habitat. This region's population of migrating and wintering gulls is considerably more diverse than the resident populations that breed in the spring and summer. The most remarkable traveler moving through the Northwest is the arctic tern. It makes round trips of more than 20,000 miles each year from breeding to wintering grounds and back again. This is no small lifetime feat; one arctic tern was recovered in the same nesting grounds where it had been banded 27 years before.

*Immature glaucous-winged gulls resting on Castle Rock*

Most species of the family enjoy settling down on protected beaches or spits to rest and socialize at midday or late afternoon. In August and September I've watched glaucous-winged and Bonaparte's gulls join common terns to form loafing aggregations on the exposed shores along estuaries. The whites and pearly grays of adult birds are radiant against the marsh floor, and the light "titters" and "cackles" of terns and Bonaparte's gulls are interwoven with the throaty calls and croaks of glaucous-winged gulls.

Immature gulls have plumage quite unlike those sported by adults. Glaucous-winged, mew, California, herring, Thayer's, western, and ring-billed gulls all go through intermediate plumage of mottled grays, browns, and whites. This cryptic coloration makes young gulls far less conspicuous, which helps them to surprise prey and avoid predators. Some of these species do not molt into adult plumage or reach sexual maturity until they are four-years old.

Members of this family are found throughout Puget Sound's different habitats. Black-legged kittiwakes normally feed in waters away from shore, occasionally wandering to inland channels to forage. Heermann's gulls prefer the channels and isolated islands of northern Puget Sound. Common, arctic, and caspian terns feed from the nearshore waters along beaches. Bonaparte's gulls often follow a foraging strategy similar to the terns, or will simply perch on

kelp to await the surfacing of small fish. They also take to the shallows to swim or walk the edge of a gentle surf where they dip for food.

Bigger gulls regularly drop down on surface-feeding fish schools, and also patrol beaches and feed opportunistically. The ubiquitous glaucous-winged gull is just as likely to be seen walking along a changing tideline seizing exposed animals as paddling through a tidal rip with Heermann's gulls. Flocks of mew gulls are commonly seen inland feeding on insects and worms in fields. Western and herring gulls, though not as numerous as glaucous-winged gulls, follow similar strategies. They are also capable of pirating the catches of other marine birds or preying on their eggs and young.

Potential oil spills pose a threat to gull and tern populations in Puget Sound, Hood Canal, the Strait of Juan de Fuca, and the San Juan Islands. The glaucous-winged gulls are the most vulnerable because they breed here. Large numbers of mew and Bonaparte's gulls that rely on these waters for food and rest during their seasonal stopovers, would also be affected by direct contact with oil or contamination of their food. The tiny arctic tern colony on Jetty Island off Everett would be especially susceptible to oil spilled near the island during breeding season.

Given the level of toxic wastes that have been observed in portions of Puget Sound, resident gulls should be tested periodically to determine the extent of contamination of birds feeding where toxins are concentrated, such as Commencement and Elliott Bays and in sanitary landfills. Toxicants like those found here have affected gulls in other areas. Ring-billed gulls appear to have died from concentrations of PCBs, dieldrin, and DDE in their brains (Sileo et al., 1977). Mirex and PCBs have been implicated in the decline of breeding populations of herring gulls in Utah (Gilman et al., 1977).

# Glaucous-winged Gull
## *Larus glaucescens*

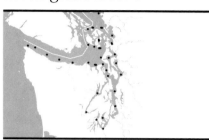

Length 56 cm (22 in)
Wingspread 138 cm (54 in)

**Status and Distribution** The glaucous-winged gull is one of the most familiar birds in Puget Sound, and is a common year-round resident and breeding bird. Immature gulls move throughout the region during the summer, while adults remain near breeding grounds.

Within the Strait of Juan de Fuca and Puget Sound there are major nesting concentrations of this species scattered over 20 large and small islands. Of these, Protection Island is the major colony with some 3,000 nesting pairs. Other important islands include Colville with 1,400 nests, Puffin Island with 600 pairs, Minor Island with 200 pairs, and Gull Rock, Bare Island, Low Island, Daughter Rock, Bird Rocks, Williamson Rocks, Flower Island, Hall Island, and Viti Rocks. Sandy Island, a human-made habitat at the north end of Swinomish Channel, has between 600 and 700 pairs of nesting gulls (Gardner, 1979).

**Food and Critical Habitat** These birds are capable scavengers (not unlike crows) and have increased here in proportion to the availability of edible refuse in landfills. They also work the intertidal zone for molluscs and crustaceans, and snap up assorted marine animals left exposed by clam diggers. The glaucous-winged gull is a formidable predator in the breeding colonies of other marine birds and is quick to take advantage of vulnerable eggs and young of cormorants, auklets, and puffins.

Although these gulls feed in virtually all marine habitats within the region, they have distinct nesting preferences and their breeding locations can be seriously disrupted by human intrusion.

# Glaucous Gull
## *Larus hyperboreus*

Length 62 cm (24 in)
Wingspread 154 cm (60 in)

**Status and Distribution** A rare winter visitor, the glaucous gull has been recorded along the Strait of Juan de Fuca, the San Juan Islands, and Puget Sound.

**Food and Critical Habitat** This large gull visits the Puget Sound region infrequently. It is usually found in the company of other scavenging gulls, particularly the common glaucous-winged. It shows up within harbors and along beaches during the winter to feed on assorted shellfish and carrion left exposed on the beaches by the tides. Its large size makes it a formidable predator, and like the glaucous-winged and western gulls, this species pirates the catches of other seabirds.

*Adult glaucous-winged gull with youngster on Colville Island*

# Western Gull
## *Larus occidentalis*

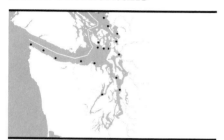

Length 54 cm (21 in)
Wingspread 141 cm (55 in)

**Status and Distribution** A permanent
resident and breeding bird on Washington's outer coast, the western gull enters the Strait of Juan de Fuca, the San
Juan Islands, and Puget Sound in small
numbers during the fall and winter. A
few of these species nest in company
with glaucous-winged gulls along the
Strait of Juan de Fuca.

**Food and Critical Habitat** Western
gulls feed on a variety of small fish,
molluscs, and crustaceans, and also
scavenge on garbage. Their prey includes the eggs and young of murres,
guillemots, and—when they can get to
them—auklets as well.

Within this region the western gull
forages over a wide range of marine
habitats, including tidal flats, salt
marshes, and beaches of rock and sand.

*Western gull seeking to
seize the catch of a whimbrel
at Dungeness Bay*

# Herring Gull
## *Larus argentatus*

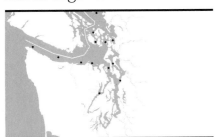

Length 51 cm (20 in)
Wingspread 141 cm (55 in)

**Status and Distribution** Along the Strait of Juan de Fuca, the San Juan Islands, and Puget Sound the herring gull is an uncommon migrant and winter resident. It is less common than the closely related Thayer's gull. In this region this species is more common on fresh water than in the Sound.

**Food and Critical Habitat** As the name suggests, herring gulls feed along entrance channels, open waters, and rocky islands where currents bring shoals of small fish to the surface. They also eat molluscs, crustaceans, and quantities of carrion. They frequently visit inland dumps to feed on garbage in company with the glaucous-winged gull.

*Immature kittiwake*

# Thayer's Gull
## *Larus thayeri*

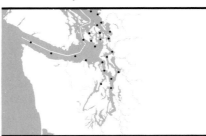

Length 51 cm (20 in)
Wingspread 141 cm (55 in)

**Status and Distribution** A rather common winter visitor and migrant, the Thayer's gull is most likely to be found in the northern portions of this region, particularly the San Juan Islands.

**Food and Critical Habitat** Although now considered a separate species, these arctic gulls are very similar in appearance and behavior to the herring gull. Although they take slightly smaller prey than their close relatives, their feeding preferences and habitat choices are the same, frequenting rocky islands and open waters. They also gather at sewage outlets to feed.

# California Gull
## *Larus californicus*

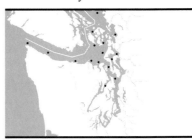

Length 44 cm (17 in)
Wingspread 133 cm (52 in)

**Status and Distribution** California gulls are migrants that are abundant from July to October and fairly common in April and May. They breed in Eastern Washington.

**Food and Critical Habitat** It was California gulls that descended from the skies over Salt Lake City, Utah to consume the hordes of black crickets that threatened the settlers' crops. On Puget Sound they scavenge and catch live prey with the best of the larger gulls. They also like to feed on smelts.

California gulls frequent sandy beaches, islands, spits, tideflats, the waters of major entrance channels, and estuaries (Gardner, 1979).

# Ring-billed Gull
## *Larus delawarensis*

Length 41 cm (16 in)
Wingspread 126 cm (49 in)

**Status and Distribution** The ring-billed gull is a common fall and spring migrant along the San Juan Islands and Puget Sound and a somewhat rare visitor throughout most of the year. It is more common on inland freshwater lakes and agricultural fields. The ring-billed breeds in Eastern Washington in colonies on islands in lakes and rivers. In Western Washington there are breeding colonies on the islands in Grays Harbor.

**Food and Critical Habitat** This medium-sized gull consumes insects during much of the year. Along the Sound it eats small fish, crustaceans, and whatever carrion and edible garbage may be available.

When present on Puget Sound the ring-billed gull ranges throughout a variety of habitats, from sandy beaches to estuarine bays, open channels, and offshore reefs.

*Ring-billed gulls*

# Mew Gull
*Larus canus*

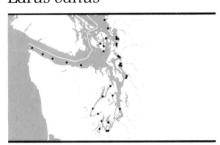

Length 36 cm (14 in)
Wingspread 108 cm (42 in)

**Status and Distribution** A common spring and fall migrant and winter resident along the Strait of Juan de Fuca, and the bays and inlets of the San Juan Islands, Puget Sound, Hood Canal, and the adjacent lowlands, mew gulls and glaucous-winged are the most abundant wintering gulls. In the north Sound, Bellingham, Samish, and Padilla Bays host mew gulls, while to the south the Stillaguamish and Nisqually Deltas are important to this species.

**Food and Critical Habitat** Mew gulls feed on insects from the flood plains and fly to the estuaries to hunt for marine animals. They forage for molluscs, crustaceans, and small fish in a variety of habitats including kelp and eelgrass beds, along jetties, rocky beaches, and islands as well as the sheltered bays of the San Juan Islands. The mew gull often settles in shallow waters over tideflats at the edge of a beach to dip for whatever edible flotsam the tide delivers.

Sandy spits, bars, and islands are important high-tide resting areas for these gulls and it is not unusual to see hundreds of mews hunkered down, beaks into the wind, restoring their energies for the next foray.

# Bonaparte's Gull
*Larus philadelphia*

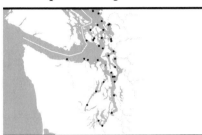

Length 28 cm (11 in)
Wingspread 82 cm (32 in)

**Status and Distribution** This species is a common migrant from March to May and July to October, along the Strait of Juan de Fuca, the San Juan Islands, Hood Canal, and on Puget Sound. Bonaparte's gulls occasionally winter here in large flocks.

Padilla and Bellingham Bays and Fisherman's Bay on Lopez Island are important gathering areas for this species. They are abundant throughout the San Juans and surrounding waters. Cultus Bay on Whidbey Island hosts large numbers of migrant Bonapartes. Dungeness Bay and Spit are also important feeding and resting locations. They are locally common in southern Puget Sound.

**Food and Critical Habitat** These delicate little gulls are effective fishers, plunging headfirst into the water for fish in much the same fashion as the common tern. Preferring the immediate offshore waters, Bonaparte's gulls gather on kelp beds to rest and to launch short fishing flights. Exposed sand bars also provide important resting areas for these gulls.

I have watched these gulls circle over marbled murrelets fishing underwater. They follow the murrelets as they drive small fish toward the surface. When the fish are within striking distance the gulls plunge and catch the prey.

# Franklin's Gull
*Larus pipixcan*

Length 28 cm (11 in)
Wingspread 90 cm (35 in)

**Status and Distribution** A periodic migrant in Puget Sound, the Franklin's gull has been observed in recent years at the Everett sewage ponds and locations along the northeastern edges of the Sound from the middle of September into early November. It is quite rare to find the Franklin's on salt water.

**Food and Critical Habitat** This gull is primarily an insectivore, but it does feed on small fish and surface invertebrates when on salt water. Its attraction to sewage ponds suggests a taste for the organisms found there.

Franklin's gulls are often seen in association with the Bonaparte's gull.

*A young mew gull*

# Heermann's Gull
*Larus heermanni*

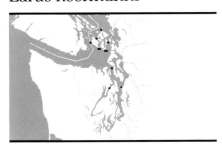

Length 38 cm (15 in)
Wingspread 128 cm (50 in)

**Status and Distribution** These birds are common nonbreeding visitors from June to November. Most Heermann's gulls concentrate in the San Juan Islands and the Strait of Juan de Fuca. During the winter months they fly south to breed in the Gulf of California. San Juan Channel is a popular feeding location for Heermann's gulls, and small flocks congregate on Colville Island and the southeast end of Lopez Island. They wander into Hood Canal and along the beaches near Edmonds and Kingston to feed.

**Food and Critical Habitat** Heermann's gulls often pursue Bonaparte's gulls, jaeger-style, to pirate their catches. As a rule, however, they feed from the open waters of entrance channels and congregate with glaucous-winged and western gulls where herring have schooled near the surface. They also eat shrimp and other crustaceans.

In the San Juan Islands, these gulls prefer rocky beaches and headlands, where they maintain resting flocks of up to several hundred birds. They also lounge on offshore rocks and floating kelp beds.

# Black-legged Kittiwake
*Rissa tridactyla*

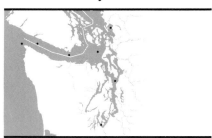

Length 35 cm (13.5 in)
Wingspread 92 cm (36 in)

**Status and Distribution** An uncommon to rare winter resident, the black-legged kittiwake has been recorded in the Strait of Juan de Fuca and in Puget Sound from Bellingham south to Olympia. It is a regular winter resident on Washington's outer coast.

**Food and Critical Habitat** Sticklebacks and other small fish are favorite foods of this species. There are old records of kittiwakes feeding on garbage heaps around Seattle, but as a rule they prefer open waters. It appears that the pressure of offshore storms brings a few of these delicately featured small gulls to the edges of Puget Sound.

# Sabine's Gull
*Xema sabini*

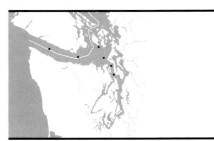

Length 28 cm (11 in)
Wingspread 77 cm (30 in)

**Status and Distribution** The Sabine's gull is a rare late summer and early fall migrant to the Strait of Juan de Fuca and portions of northern Puget Sound. A few of these miniature gulls regularly visit Admiralty Inlet and the west side of Whidbey Island (Gardner, 1979).

**Food and Critical Habitat** The Sabine's gull is normally found off shore, where it plucks small fish and crustaceans from the surface. In some parts of its range it takes to the mudflats and has been described as running about "like a shorebird."

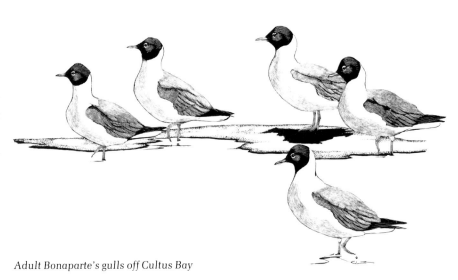

*Adult Bonaparte's gulls off Cultus Bay*

# Caspian Tern
*Sterna caspia*

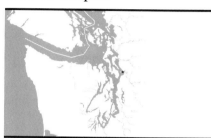

Length 51 cm (20 in)
Wingspread 136 cm (53 in)

**Status and Distribution** Breeding on islands in Grays Harbor and Willapa Bay on Washington's southern coasts, this bird is an uncommon summer and fall visitor to Puget Sound. A modest increase in the 1960s and 1970s in the state portends a breeding population in Puget Sound, possibly on Sandy Island off Swinomish Channel (Gardner, 1979).

**Food and Critical Habitat** The Caspian is the largest of the terns. It flies with grace and authority, sometimes plunging from 30 feet to strike the water and retrieve fish that smaller terns can't catch.

Small groups of Caspians sometimes rest on sandy spits or beaches. When they take to the air their size and strong flight are memorable. With a few pumps of their wings they are under way, cutting across the surf to open waters, where they quickly shift direction with consummate ease as they scout for a meal.

*A pair of Caspian terns*

# Black Tern
*Chlidonias niger*

Length 23 cm (9 in)
Wingspread 90 cm (35 in)

**Status and Distribution** The black tern is a rare winter visitor to Puget Sound in late summer or early fall. This species breeds in Eastern Washington.

**Food and Critical Habitat** During its infrequent visits to Puget Sound the black tern occasionally joins common terns to hunt for fish near shore.

# Common Tern
*Sterna hirundo*

Length 36 cm (14 in)
Wingspread 79 cm (31 in)

**Status and Distribution** These birds are fairly common migrants in spring from late April into May and from August to October. They are abundant along the Strait of Juan de Fuca and throughout the San Juans during their fall migration, which appears to peak in September and October. Fisherman's and Mud Bays on Lopez Island and the waters peripheral to Cypress Island are good examples of resting locations important to common terns. The estuaries of the Skagit and Nisqually Deltas and Dungeness Bay also provide feeding habitat for these migrants.

**Food and Critical Habitat** Feeding in the immediate offshore waters and in open channels, these buoyant birds dive for small fish including sand lances, pipefish, and herring, as well as shrimps.

# Arctic Tern
*Sterna paradisaea*

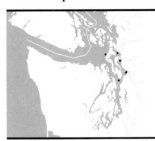

Length 38 cm (15 in)
Wingspread 79 cm (31 in)

**Status and Distribution** This species is a breeding bird and a rare migrant in Puget Sound. There is a small nesting colony of arctic terns on Jetty Island near Everett (Gardner, 1979). Five pairs were on nests in 1979.

**Food and Critical Habitat** Near their breeding island, arctic terns feed on small fish from the shallow waters over tidal flats and adjacent to sandy beaches. They also fish entrance channels.

*Common terns over Fisherman's Bay on Lopez Island*

Common tern "scouting" for prey

# Murres and Puffins
## *Alcidae*

One afternoon I was snorkeling along Lopez Island's southeast edges when suddenly I found myself surrounded by a school of smelt. Their bodies glittered like foil, and their tails whipped frantically. As I stretched out my gloved hand, they shimmered out of reach. When I dove from the surface the school broke and scattered only to regroup again, far above me.

Entering the edges of a kelp bed, I grasped a buoyant cord to check my movement, and the bright tinsel cloud drifted on. As I watched them, an animal form broke into the outer edges of the shoal. Its wings pumping steadily, a rhinoceros auklet maneuvered—almost herded—a portion of the school away from the larger mass of fish. Some of them darted toward a haven of sea grass on the sandy bottom, but the bird intercepted them and they turned back to the surface. Accelerating its wing strokes, the hunter was into their midst and snapped one up.

Although the entire episode lasted no more than thirty seconds, I remember it as one would a well-choreographed ballet. The participants were finely tuned and rehearsed, one for escape and the other for pursuit. In this act, the hunter had the edge.

Alcids have evolved a form and musculature that are fitted as much for underwater propulsion as for flight. Their ability to use their wings as paddles is a chief characteristic of all alcids, yet they have other distinguishing physical qualities as well. Their beaks are particularly varied and have, to some degree, been influenced by their feeding preferences. The very distinctive bills of tufted puffins and rhinoceros auklets are employed in their courtship displays. The heft and base width of the bills enable these species to transport many fish at once so they can capture prey far from their nests.

Common murres and pigeon guillemots have narrow bills. They feed closer to their nests and transport only one fish at a time. The smallest of the alcid family breeding in Washington, the Cassin's auklet, is the most distant feeder, and returns to its nest only at dusk and evening. With its spoon-shaped bill, it can hold quantities of semidigested macroplankton. A gular pouch develops during the breeding season, which permits additional food storage.

The tongues of alcids are also specialized. Those of the tufted puffin and rhinoceros auklet are partially cornified, which helps them hold fish against the denticles on the roof of their beaks. With the captured fish in this position they can still open the lower mandible and seize additional prey. A puffin or rhinoceros auk-

let can transport fish on both sides of its beak, catching fish first on one side and then the other while holding the captured prey in place. A Cassin's auklet uses its broad and fleshy tongue to compress small food particles downward into a throat pouch for temporary storage.

The feet of some alcids are used for more than surface swimming or an occasional awkward amble. Puffins, guillemots, and Cassin's auklets excavate cavities for nesting. Their beaks are used to remove stubborn stones, but it is their long, sharp, angled toenails that make them effective diggers. Rhinoceros auklets' burrows may meander more than three meters. Cassin's auklets, however, rarely tunnel more than a meter before forming the snug nesting chamber.

As in other families of marine birds, alcid feeding habits tend to separate individual species and reduce competition for food. This zonation is most pronounced during the breeding season. Pigeon guillemots feed in shallow nearshore waters while murres prefer open channels between islands. Tufted puffins and rhinoceros auklets typically feed in the vast stretches of water of the Strait of Juan de Fuca as well as entrance channels. Cassin's auklets wander still further to open waters where they capture euphasiids.

These birds also exploit food resources at different depths. The largest and heaviest of the family, the murre, can dive down to deeper schools of fish, averaging some 40 seconds under water. The Cassin's auklet and marbled murrelet are shallow divers, remaining submerged for much shorter periods of time.

Pressures of predation also affect alcid behavior. Some of the smallest members of this clan tend to be crepuscular or nocturnal when returning to feed their young. Such is the case with the Cassin's and rhinoceros auklets. Awkward and vulnerable on land, they and their exposed broods are favored prey of the powerful glaucous-winged and western gulls.

Burrowing reduces the effects of such predation, but one family member has developed still another strategy. The marbled murrelet flies inland and nests in old-growth timber, preferring a hollow tree to a burrow on island ground. The flightless youngsters apparently reach the sea by floating down the nearest river. Durable and buoyant, they move through white water and calm, eventually entering estuaries where they can begin feeding. Once in these waters, they can dive to escape predators.

A final word regarding the welfare of this family must stress the importance of not only protected feed-

*Tufted puffin catching fish*
*while holding previous catches with tongue*

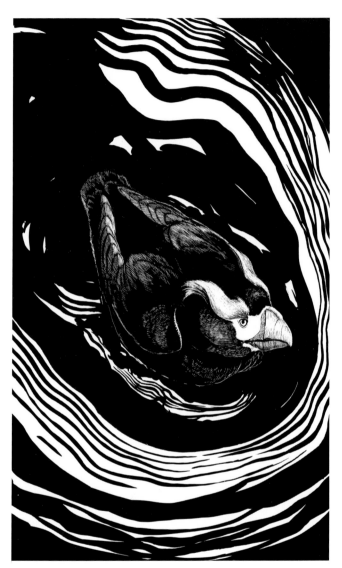

*Resting tufted puffin*

ing waters, but breeding habitat as well. The more remote islands and cliffs of the region have traditionally been favored sites for nesting. An absence of mammals has made these locations attractive and suitable. Such habitat is becoming increasingly rare. Human activity and pets are the chief threat to these retreats. On Smith Island, for example, a pet dog once killed nearly ten percent of the rhinoceros auklet colony.

Development pressure on Protection Island caused continued erosion of suitable nesting ground for the thousands upon thousands of birds breeding there. (Violet Spit, home to a major glaucous-winged gull colony, is also eyed by developers.) The presence of wandering sightseers on Protection Island has sent brooding puffins and cormorants into flight, leaving eggs and young exposed to chilling or predation from gulls.

A resident Game Department biologist on the island during summer helps reduce human impact but won't save this exceptional breeding retreat for marine birds. Even the acquisition of 15 percent of the property by The Nature Conservancy, later obtained by the Game Department, has done little to stem the cumulative effect of human presence. Only concerted action by a concerned public and state and federal agencies will ensure that this extraordinary natural resource endures. Federal land acquisition on Protection Island is still planned and the remarkable effort by the local Audubon chapter to purchase single lots sustains the hope this extraordinary marine bird nursery will be saved.

In their quest for food, these birds are exposed to yet another threat to their welfare. If an oil slick were to drift into foraging areas, feeding alcids would be dining and surfacing continually through oil. The birds would likely ingest hydrocarbons directly while feeding or attempting to preen their feathers (Miller et al., 1978).

# Common Murre
## *Uria aalge*

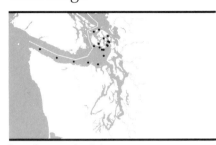

Length 36 cm (14 in)

**Status and Distribution**  A permanent resident of Washington's coast, common murres are most often found along the Strait of Juan de Fuca, in the San Juan Islands, and in Puget Sound during the fall and winter. As early as late August small flocks of murres assemble to feed in Haro and Rosario Straits and the channels throughout the San Juan Islands.

Murres breed only on the outer coast. There are large nesting concentrations at Grenville Island (3,800 young), Grenville Arch, Split and Willoughby Rocks (Gardner, 1979).

**Food and Critical Habitat**  Murres dine in open waters of entrance channels and offshore reefs in search of sand lances, herring, smelts, and some bottomfish.

They incubate eggs during June and July and require steep ledges for their nesting colonies. They are particularly sensitive to human disturbance along the tops of nesting cliffs during the breeding season.

Although oiling is a potential danger to these birds, my observations suggest that a more immediate danger to the murre population results from hundreds of them drowning each year in fishing nets in northern Puget Sound and the Strait of Juan de Fuca. This conclusion is drawn from interviews with fishermen and in late summer finding beaches in the San Juan Islands littered with the bodies of these murres and rhinoceros auklets.

*A small flock of pigeon guillemots in breeding plumage*

*A marbled murrelet in breeding plumage*

# Pigeon Guillemot
## *Cepphus columba*

Length 27 cm (10.5 in)

# Marbled Murrelet
## *Brachyramphus marmoratus*

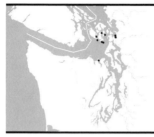

Length 21 cm (8 in)

**Status and Distribution** The pigeon guillemot is a resident and breeding bird along the Strait of Juan de Fuca, Hood Canal, the San Juan Islands, and Puget Sound. It is estimated that approximately 1,235 pairs of guillemots breed within this region, not including Canadian waters (Manuwal et al., 1979). They concentrate on Smith, Protection (hundreds are seen in the spring), Sentinel, and Flower Islands (255 adults and young), and Castle and Skip Jack Rocks (Gardner, 1979). Southward through the Sound, scattered nesting occurs in bluffs on the east sides of Bainbridge, Vashon, Fox, and Anderson Islands. Discovery Park in Seattle also hosts breeding guillemots (Gardner, 1979).

**Food and Critical Habitat** These birds prefer small fish, including blennies, sculpins, sand lances and smelts. They fish the shallow waters of bays and along beaches, and work kelp beds along the edges of offshore rocks and reefs. Occasionally they feed with other alcids in the open waters of entrance channels.

Pigeon guillemots nest in rock crevices of cliffs, hollows in bluffs of sand or clay, and beneath beach logs. These birds are very sensitive to human intrusion.

**Status and Distribution** A common migrant and winter resident, the marbled murrelet is found in waters along the Strait of Juan de Fuca, the San Juan Islands, and Puget Sound. Actual nesting locations of this species in Washington remain a mystery. The breeding population is estimated to be about 800 pairs (Manuwal et al., 1979).

Adult birds are found feeding in Puget Sound throughout the year with larger concentrations during the fall and winter. Flocks of hundreds of murrelets occasionally gather in Padilla Bay in winter, and late summer populations assemble in the San Juan National Wildlife Refuge.

**Food and Critical Habitat** Feeding away from shore, these compact little birds dive for sand lances, sea perch, and other small schooling fish. Some small crustaceans are also eaten. Open waters of entrance channels off rocky shores or over reefs are important feeding locations for the marbled murrelet. They also occupy estuaries and protected bays.

The nests of marbled murrelets that have been located suggest that they depend on hollows within the trees of old-growth forests. As the old-growth forest goes so may go a significant portion of Puget Sound's population of breeding murrelets. At higher elevations they may use ground burrows.

# Ancient Murrelet
*Synthliboramphus antiquus*

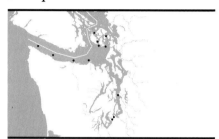

Length 21 cm (8 in)

# Cassin's Auklet
*Ptychoramphus aleuticus*

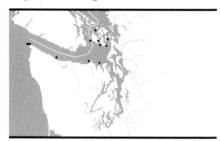

Length 18 cm (7 in)

# Rhinoceros Auklet
*Cerorhinca monocerata*

Length 29 cm (11.5 in)

**Status and Distribution** This species is a winter resident in the Strait of Juan de Fuca, the San Juan Islands, and Puget Sound. Sightings of ancient murrelets have become numerous in recent years. They are usually found from November until midwinter, and occasionally remain here into May.

These birds are regularly observed off Discovery Park in Seattle and are found southward to The Narrows during the late fall and early winter. The San Juan Islands host large concentrations of ancient murrelets (Gardner, 1979).

**Food and Critical Habitat** These strongly patterned birds prefer euphasiids and small fish taken in open-water habitats well off beaches and in large entrance channels. Prey species include sand lances, smelts, shiner perch, and rockfish (Gardner, 1979).

They fly in little flocks that dive directly into the water from flight. They move in swimming lines like miniature murres, all the while calling in high-pitched squeals.

**Status and Distribution** A resident breeding species on Tatoosh, Destruction, and Carroll Islands off Washington's outer coast, Cassin's auklets are uncommon in winter within the Strait of Juan de Fuca, the San Juan Islands, and Puget Sound, although feeding groups do appear. Admiralty Inlet frequently hosts wintering groups of birds and they have been observed off Protection Island during the breeding season (Gardner, 1979). Whether Cassin's auklets breed in the San Juan Islands is yet to be determined.

**Food and Critical Habitat** Euphasiids comprise a large portion of this bird's diet and that of the young during the breeding season. They also eat copepods and small fish (less than an inch long).

An excavatable substrate is required for these little alcids to dig their nesting burrows.

**Status and Distribution** A breeding bird in Washington, the rhinoceros auklet is common during late spring and into the summer and fall in the Strait of Juan de Fuca, the San Juan Islands and northern Puget Sound. In the winter large numbers of rhinoceros auklets probably retire to the waters well off Washington's outer coast. Some remain, however, to winter in the southern Sound (Paulson, 1980). Admiralty Inlet, Discovery Bay, and the waters north of Protection and Smith islands are fished regularly by this species during the summer months.

The waters of San Juan Channel, along Haro Strait, and east into Rosario Strait are fished by thousands of birds during summer months. They return to their burrows on Protection Island at dusk and darkness to feed their young. A breeding population estimated to be over 17,800 pairs exists on Protection Island. Smith Island supports a much smaller breeding colony, and a few birds also nest on Tatoosh Island (Manuwal et al., 1979). Burrows are occupied from May into early August.

**Food and Critical Habitat** Sand lances, anchovies, herring, and surf smelts are important staples of this species' diet. The birds feed in open coastal waters, over reefs, estuaries, and entrance channels.

*Ancient murrelets*

*An adult diving rhinoceros auklet
closing in on a school of herring*

# Tufted Puffin
## *Lunda cirrhata*

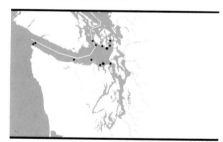

Length 32 cm (12.5 in)

**Status and Distribution** These birds
are uncommon summer residents along
the Strait of Juan de Fuca and within
the San Juan Islands. Tufted puffins
breed on a few isolated islands where
they can burrow in the substrate or
where cavities already exist.

The largest concentrations of puffins
in this state remain along the outer
coast. These groups may be the last of
this species in Washington State if nesting habitat is lost in Puget Sound and
the herring decline.

Within the Strait of Juan de Fuca,
Colville and Protection Islands still
provide nesting habitat for breeding
puffins. Feeding areas of importance
include Haro Strait, San Juan Passage,
and Rosario Strait.

*"Lounging" tufted puffins on Colville Island*

**Food and Critical Habitat** These
bright-beaked alcids prefer smelts, herring, sardines, and other small fish, as
well as sea urchins, molluscs, and
squids. They feed in large entrance
channels and offshore waters. Occasionally, puffins join auklets and
murres where tidal rips cause upwelling water to bring shoals of feeding fish
near the surface. The alcid activity in
turn attracts gulls, loons, and cormorants, which then join in the feeding.

Like other marine birds that breed
on islands, puffins are sensitive to intrusion.

# Owls
## *Strigidae*

The delta of the Nisqually River is a flat wedge of sediment settled between high bluffs. From the outer dike tiny water rivulets fringe its edge spreading out like a hundred little fingers. From where I stood the distant highway was invisible and its noise muffled; there was nothing to suggest that this was the 20th century. Thousands of wintering ducks—wigeons, mallards, and pintails—shifted restlessly from one feeding waterway to another. Marsh hawks flap-glided forward and back over hedgerows, dropping occasionally to snatch at voles prowling beneath the flattened grasses. A rough-legged hawk sat puffed out and sleepy-eyed high in a distant cottonwood.

A hard rain began pressing the grass down still further and a blue and brown world changed to shades of gray. McAllister Creek was pelted into a rage of ripples and the estuary surface seethed in blackness. Far out on the flat perched on top of a beached snag was a snowy owl, swiveling her head from side to side, eyes wide and searching. Something beckoned and she pushed off, dropped low to the water, and flew toward a distant headland. Cresting a tussock she disturbed a trio of male wigeons from their feeding. Ignoring them, she flew on, gathered momentum, and finally disappeared into the gloom.

They come each year to Puget Sound, sometimes in such numbers that six to eight birds can be seen hunting along a single stretch of beach. A severe year in the Arctic, when summer is late and there are food shortages in the fall, coupled with a high population of owls, will sometimes bring hundreds of these phantoms to Washington's coasts and open islands. The ones that compete effectively with resident predators and find sufficient food return northward to produce new generations.

The snowy and short-eared owls are the only two members of this family that regularly exploit the food resources of the salt marshes and associated beach habitats. The snowy is an opportunistic predator, and will feed on small mammals, injured game birds, and even carcasses of beached marine mammals. One winter I spotted snowy owls along the open coast feeding on murres that had been crippled by oiling (Angell, 1974). It was interesting to note how quickly these predators had learned to take advantage of this food source, though ingesting oil off the murres' bodies was ultimately a danger to the owls' health.

Snowy owls are very conspicuous in this region as they seem content to sit out in the worst storms. They, too, have their limits, but they are durable birds when it comes to staying warm. Their feathering is remarkably weather-resistant. Contour feathers shed moisture and down feathers beneath provide insulation that is nearly impenetrable to rain and chill. Their heels and toes are covered with a specialized feathering more like hair than feathers. It covers both top and bottom so that little if any heat is lost from this point of exposure.

Although owls must remain warm, they must also cool off on occasion. For a bird as heavily feathered as a snowy owl this is not an easy process. One winter when temperatures along northern Puget Sound reached into the sixties, a group of snowy owls gathered in a cabbage field on Samish Island and tried a number of cooling strategies. Although their white feathers reflect rather than absorb sunlight, cooling off required active tactics. Some owls stood, wings partially extended, letting the air circulate over the patches of exposed skin beneath their wings. Other owls fluffed out and settled onto the cool ground. All of them were breathing heavily, the way a dog pants to cool off.

All owls can see well in daylight, but only a few of them choose to hunt during the day. The snowy owl has no choice, in the far north in the summer it must hunt in nearly continuous light. The short-eared owl forages at all hours and in much the same manner as a marsh hawk, flying buoyantly along hedgerows and dikes. It is this species that occasionally shows a sociality not readily found among other members of this family. On one occasion, far out on a delta, I came upon at least 20 of these birds apparently roosting communally amid depressions of marsh grass. When they flushed it was almost impossible to follow a single bird. They wheeled around us, gradually drifting farther down the marsh and disappearing against the browns, grays, and cream colors of nearshore meadows. Their roosting location discouraged most approaches: there was a moat of water around it when the tide was in, and a disagreeable expanse of mud when it was out.

Loss of habitat or contamination from oil that affects birds and small mammals in marine environments affects these predators, for their survival is inextricably linked to that of their prey.

# Snowy Owl
*Nyctea scandiaca*

Length 51 cm (to 20 in)
Wingspread 141 cm (to 55 in)

**Status and Distribution** Occurring in much of Washington, the snowy owl is a cyclical migrant and winter resident, concentrating in peak visitation years along the coastal beaches, the Strait of Juan de Fuca, the San Juan Islands, and Puget Sound from late November into April.

Snowy owls migrate to Washington's coasts almost every year. They normally frequent estuaries and mudflats from the Nooksack southward to Samish, Padilla, and Skagit Bays, where the greatest number of owls congregate. Dungeness Spit hosts snowy owls and in years of heavier migration they wander deep into Puget Sound to hunt along the Nisqually estuary.

**Food and Critical Habitat** Along our coasts the snowy owl captures ducks, gulls, grebes, loons, alcids, other owls, and songbirds. They also catch voles where grasses grow adjacent to mudflats.

# Short-eared Owl
*Asio flammeus*

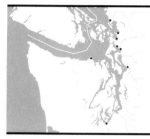

Length 33 cm (to 13 in)
Wingspread 105 cm (to 41 in)

**Status and Distribution** A permanent resident of Washington, the short-eared owl breeds on both sides of the Cascades. It is most common along Puget Sound in winter. The mouths of the Nooksack, Skagit, Stillaguamish, and Nisqually Rivers provide particularly important feeding habitat for this species. The Tacoma tideflats have hosted breeding short-eared owls (Jewett et al., 1953).

**Food and Critical Habitat** This diurnal and crepuscular hunter consumes enormous numbers of small mammals. In summer, insects are a large part of its diet. It hunts the grassy edges of salt marshes and along dikes facing the estuaries of the Sound. Salt marsh islands of dry open land where low grass cover and wild roses grow are important retreats for nesting and breeding birds.

*A short-eared owl flies over a salt marsh*

# Kingfishers
*Alcedinidae*

Throughout the Puget Sound region, along shores and salt marshes, and crouched on the edges of wharves, one finds the contemplative, short-necked, dagger-beaked kingfisher. This is the single representative in the Pacific Northwest of a family of 90 species.

Although its direct flight does not have the buoyant lilt of the common tern, it shares similar fishing strategies when in flight. Both species patrol just off shore over shallow salt water, alternately hovering and flying with their heads down, surveying stretches of tidewater. When they spot a fish, they plummet headlong into the water, often plunging below the surface to retrieve prey.

A fishing foray comes to an abrupt end, however, if one kingfisher intrudes on another's territory. Clashes at territorial boundaries usually start a series of "hell-bent" chases, accompanied by rattling alarm calls. With remarkable precision and timing, they thread the pilings under wharfs, hurl over water, and race through fringes of forest in full chase.

The vigor with which kingfishers protect their territory is most intense with the onset of breeding, when nesting habitat is defended along with feeding waters. The birds excavate sandy bluffs using their great bills like spades and feet like scoops. Nesting tunnels may extend from only a few feet to up to ten feet into a bank, ending in a chamber where they lay four to six eggs.

Kingfishers feeding in bays and along beaches where boating activity is intense could suffer exposure to oiling during their intermittent dips for fish. If a major spill occurred, it would likely contaminate fishing grounds.

*Female belted kingfisher*

## Belted Kingfisher
*Ceryle alcyon*

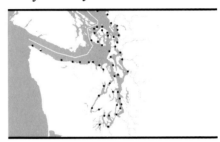

Length 31 cm (12 in)

**Status and Distribution**  The belted kingfisher is a common year-round resident and breeding bird throughout Washington, including the Strait of Juan de Fuca, the San Juan Islands, Hood Canal, and Puget Sound.

**Food and Critical Habitat**  This compact fishing bird consumes sand lances, herring, perch, and other small fishes, as well as small crabs in the saltwater environment. Rich shallows in estuaries are important feeding areas for kingfishers, as are the sheltered bays throughout the San Juan Islands. They are quick to exploit human-made structures like dock railings and walks, pilings, and edges of abandoned buildings as hunting vantage points.

# Ravens and Crows
## *Corvidae*

In January 1979, my family and I sat snug around a wood stove in a cabin on Lopez Island watching a parade of ten-foot swells rolling up Rosario Strait. Throughout our week's stay the cabin shuddered and moaned painfully as the wind tore into its openings and over its edges. It wasn't until we left the island that we were to learn Seattle had been plunged into darkness by the long storm, and the frenzied winds had snapped the Hood Canal floating bridge into pieces, sending more than half of it to the bottom.

Although we had a vista of nearly 180 degrees, there were no birds to be seen. Rafts of wintering ducks and gulls had taken refuge in leeward bays. Small passerines had retreated to deeper forests. We could only guess where the hawks and eagles had gone, and imagined them compressed against the face of some great cliff or tree, protected from the devouring maw of the wind.

As we layered ourselves in jackets and hats and stepped outside, the winds pitched a meringue of sea foam up from the shore. Amid the wind's howl and the debris-filled air we were surprised to first hear and then see three ravens fly out over Watmough Head heading for the north end of Whidbey Island some ten miles distant. "Krawk, krawk," was their periodic call, and had we not been watching them we would have looked behind us, for the colliding winds snatched their voices away then delivered them from another direction.

They were about two miles off shore and appeared to be going nowhere. They stroked desperately, colliding again and again with the incredible fortress of wind. We were waiting for them to return from this folly when one bird discovered some passage and led the others through. They squeezed between wedges of wind, slid down the back side of some eddy of air, and continued their journey.

When they reached midchannel I went to the cabin for my binoculars. In the glasses' magnification their silhouettes were set off against an eruption of clouds flooding the eastern sky. Again and still again they seemed repulsed, only to find some narrow path momentarily open up to allow them through. It was 30 minutes after we first saw them that they were lost to the Whidbey woods. I wondered then, and have wondered since, what powerful siren called them across the raging edge of the storm.

Where marine habitats have been lost and dramatically changed the more specialized species like the black oystercatcher or tufted puffin have declined in Puget Sound over the past 25 years. But habitat disruption in some ways favors crows, and over the same interval their populations have increased in the region. Omniverous, intelligent, and aggressive, crows are quick to exploit the food resources of picnic beaches and trailer and camping parks that have been opened up to accommodate the ever-increasing pressure for outdoor recreation. Our trash may be a crow's main course and our presence discourages less tolerant species from feeding and breeding in locations no longer remote from human activity.

Crows form feeding, breeding, and roosting aggregations throughout Puget Sound, but the raven is far less gregarious. It is in large part common only to the northern portions of Puget Sound. The common crow joins the raven in scavenging, and these bold black birds can be seen along the shoreline retrieving dead young from seabird colonies or pulling scraps from an animal carcass washed in on the tide. Like gulls they follow clam diggers and snap up whatever has been left in exposed trenches. Sometimes, they drop clams, "gull fashion," on hard surfaces to crack the shells. One crow I observed went one step further; it dropped them on a road used by ferry traffic. Once the traffic had cleared, the crow dropped down to the road to consume his "minced" clams (Angell, 1978).

Ravens and crows are ideally built to fulfill the role of generalist feeders along Puget Sound. They are strong fliers and can survey beaches and island bird colonies all in a morning's time. Their powerful beaks can dispatch small mammals, probe crevices, hammer, pry, and gape. A slight hook at the beak's tip facilitates tearing, pulling, and stripping. Both ravens and crows have throat pouches for transporting food, and the raven in particular caches unconsumed food to retrieve later.

## Common Raven
*Corvus corax*

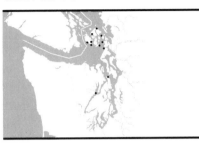

Length 54 cm (21 in)
Wingspread 128 cm (50 in)

**Status and Distribution**  A permanent resident of Western Washington, the common raven shows a distinct preference for marine locations. It breeds in the San Juan Islands and along the Strait of Juan de Fuca; few ravens are found south of Admiralty Inlet.

**Food and Critical Habitat**  In some parts of their range, ravens team up to flush seabirds from their nests, and then return to seize eggs and young. It is normal, however, for them to forage opportunistically, taking at first light what the tide has deposited on the beach the night before. They strip carcasses of animals washed ashore and after feeding often cache whatever they carry away.

Ravens along our coasts have learned to fear humankind and though easily seen when aloft or along a beach, they retreat to old-growth forests and remote cliff faces to breed. Occasionally, a pair constructs a nest in an abandoned building.

This species is often blamed for preying on the young of range animals and poultry when it was most likely a newborn that died of exposure or another predator that did the killing and the raven was simply feeding from the carcass.

## Common Crow
*Corvus brachyrhynchos*

Length 44 cm (17 in)
Wingspread 90 cm (35 in)

**Status and Distribution**  A permanent resident along the Strait of Juan de Fuca, the San Juan Islands, Hood Canal, and Puget Sound, the common crow has fared well in this era of disrupted habitats. Its population has increased considerably in the past decade as more specialized birds give way to those species like the crow that can exploit changes.

**Food and Critical Habitat**  In Puget Sound, footprints of crows are often found mixed with those of shorebirds and dabbling ducks along beaches. They turn shells to test their soundness, snatch up small crabs, and do some shallow probing when the surface appears promising. Like the raven and assorted gull species, crows regularly scavenge refuse along the beaches. Inland, sanitary landfills have broadened the food base of these birds.

Today, to some degree, the presence of crows in large numbers is a reflection of our own actions. If we are concerned that they displace other species we should reduce or eliminate the activity contributing to their increase. The crow cannot be blamed for retrieving garbage or preying on young seabirds exposed because people have flushed the adults from the nest. Perhaps the increase in the populations of the highly adaptable crow is an important message to all who wish to retain the rich diversity of marine bird species within the regions of greater Puget Sound.

*Three crows*

*Three ravens over Rosario Strait*

# Marine Mammals

The story of the marine mammals of Puget Sound begins with the origins of marine mammals themselves, for there are none which are unique to this area, and there are few which have not lived here at some time. Indeed, the return of mammals to a marine way of life 20 to 60 million years ago could well have been in a place or places topographically similar to Puget Sound, where inshore and inland waters are alternately stirred by winds and tides and radiated by the sun.

Eighty million years ago the marine food chain was capped by large predatory fishes, reptiles, and marine birds that were ancestors of loons, grebes, and pelicans. At that time mammals dominated the food webs on land, but they had not yet ventured into the sea. Imagine, for a moment, that you are a hairy and hungry creature on the shore of waters that teem with life. On land, there is intense competition for the food resources, and hungry carnivorous beasts that may consider you their next meal. There is a tremendous advantage for you to wade into the water—perhaps a little bit at a time—to enjoy the food and protection it offers. Over millenia, the creatures that possessed the inclination and anatomy to do so eventually became adapted primarily to the water and rarely came out on land. Some of them eventually lost all need for legs to walk upon, and never again returned to land. Some groups of these mammals—desmostylians, cetotheres, and sirenians—appeared and disappeared with the ages, while others have remained as part of a continuously evolving scenario of marine creatures in the waters of Puget Sound.

### The Cetaceans—Whales, Dolphins, and Porpoises

Among the very first marine mammals were the whales, dolphins and porpoises of the order Cetacea. They evolved very rapidly once the initial step was made into the water. It is not known precisely when or where this step took place, or even whether more than one type of land creature concurrently accomplished this feat. What is known from fossil evidence, however, is that 55 million years ago there were primitive, completely aquatic cetaceans living in all marine waters of the world, and some were venturing into major rivers and lakes.

At that time the entire Pacific Northwest was under water and Puget Sound was only a deep trench. But there were no doubt similar inshore habitats wherein some cetaceans evolved specialized roles, while others tended toward the open seas. Among the cetacea

that now occur in Puget Sound are species of both suborders: Odontoceti, the "toothed" whales, and Mysticeti, the baleen whales. The names are derived from the Greek words for teeth, *odontos*; moustache, *mystax*; and whale, *ketos*.

Mysticetes feed on small schooling fishes and invertebrates, which they filter from the water through hundreds of baleen plates—parallel ridges of cornified epithelium with a fringed inner edge—that grow from the roof of the mouth. This anatomical specialty permits them to feed on organisms very close to the primary production level in the sea. Typically, seasonal "blooms" of their prey species—such as krill—occur in the high latitudes during spring and summer. Most mysticete whales therefore migrate to feeding areas when food is available, and migrate to temperate or tropical regions in the winter to breed and calve.

The mysticete cetaceans are taxonomically divided into three families comprising nine species, which are differentiated by anatomy and physical characteristics. The family Balaenidae includes the right whales and bowhead whales, which have a high arched rostrum and no dorsal fin. The Balaenopteridae family—called rorquals—includes the finner whales and humpbacks, which have a dorsal fin and numerous pleats of skin on the throat. The family Eschrichtiidae has only one living member, the gray whale, which has a slightly arched rostrum and no dorsal fin. All three families are represented in the Pacific Northwest, but due to extensive whaling in the past some species are very rare in occurrence. Only the latter two families are represented in Puget Sound at present.

The odontocete cetaceans are taxonomically divided into six families comprising approximately 68 different species. The family Physeteridae includes the sperm whales, which have functional teeth only on the lower jaw. Ziphiidae, the beaked whales, have dentition that is characteristically reduced to two or four functional teeth on the lower jaw. Monodontidae, the narwhal and beluga whales, are unique in that they have completely adapted to the arctic environment. Platanistidae, the freshwater dolphins, are a primitive looking group that has secondarily adapted to fresh water. Delphinidae are the marine dolphins—of wide and varied description—including pilot whales and killer whales. Phocoenidae are the porpoises, which have spade-shaped teeth and characteristically blunt foreheads. There have been occurrences of all these families except Platanistidae in Puget Sound, but at the present time only the Delphinidae and Phocoenidae are regularly found here.

**Pinnipedia—The Fin-footed Mammals**

Long, long after cetaceans had evolved to be the supreme creatures of the sea, several other surges of land mammals headed toward the water, perhaps to avoid competition and predation on land, or perhaps to exploit an amphibious niche that the cetaceans had passed quickly through. Whatever the reason, about 20 million years ago some of these carnivorous mammals ventured into the marine environment. They evolved paddle-shaped feet for mobility in water, but still retained the ability to move about on land. These creatures are the fin-footed mammals—seals, sea lions, and walruses—of the order Pinnipedia (from the Latin *pinna* meaning feather and *pes* meaning foot). Pinnipeds are found in all oceans and seas of the world and even in freshwater lakes. Several of these species presently inhabit the marine waters of Puget Sound, and others have lived here in the past.

The order Pinnipedia is composed of three families of carnivorous mammals: the Odobenidae, whose sole surviving representative is the walrus; the Phocidae, which are the true seals; and the Otariidae, the eared seals, sea lions, and fur seals. Among this trio, sea lions are distinguished from seals by physical characteristics and behavioral traits, and walruses are easily distinguished by their tusks. Sea lions have external ear pinnae, their front flippers are much larger than their hind flippers, and their hind flippers rotate forward enabling them to shuffle along on all fours when on land. Seals, on the other hand, with smaller and nonrotatable flippers can only hunch along on their bellies, scratching at the ground with their claws.

In the water, sea lions are almost continuously on the move, their bodies stretched out horizontally, undulating at the surface as they breathe. Seals, on the other hand, generally bob to the surface vertically, and drift with the tide while breathing. Sea lions are also noisier creatures than seals, barking or roaring while hauled out, while seals are usually silent, except for an occasional sneeze or bleating sound.

Pinnipeds spend the majority of their life at sea, feeding on fish and invertebrates or migrating to and from feeding areas. All, however, must return to land or ice to rest, breed, and give birth.

The places which are regularly used for breeding and pupping are known as rookeries; those used for resting are known as haulout areas. Both rookeries and haulouts are essential to the survival of these animals. Although one location may serve both purposes, such a site must be conveniently close to food resources, yet strategically remote from potential disturbance by land predators or human intervention and disturbance. A rookery may also be used as a haulout area, giving it quite a distinctive smell and lived in appearance. Haulouts, however, may be only temporarily used locations, and even buoys, jetties, or moored boats may provide a weary seal or sea lion a temporary rest site.

In Puget Sound, islands and islets are the usual rookery sites, and some are used by pinnipeds year after year. Puget Sound is still blessed with a number of such sites and with a rich and varied bounty of marine mammals. The species accounts that follow are intended to help you recognize the marine animals that occur in Puget Sound's inland waters, and the areas and conditions critical to their existence and well-being.

# Seals
## Phocidae

There are two species of the Phocidae family found in Puget Sound, the harbor seal and the elephant seal. The smaller and most common is the harbor seal. It is a pig-sized creature with short brownish fur that is often dotted with a camouflage pattern of dark and light spots and rings. Harbor seals are in the area year-round and are usually seen at low tide, when they haul out on small islets and exposed rocks. They do not venture far from the water's edge, and will stampede clumsily back into the water at the slightest indication of danger.

In the water, a harbor seal can be identified by the low profile of its gently rounded head, a broad snout, and enormous dark eyes that blink inquisitively at intruders. A seal normally disappears quickly and silently, leaving only a small swirl as it sinks beneath the surface. If startled, however, it may roll quickly forward and dive, its rear flippers briefly waving in the air, frogman style.

Beneath the surface, a harbor seal reveals its superb adaptation to a marine existence. Its breathing stops, the heart rate slows, the pupils of the eyes dilate to adjust to the reduced light, and its hearing compensates to match the acoustic impedance of the water. Powerful hind flippers propel it like a living torpedo. With subtle body and flipper movements it turns and glides wherever the brain commands. The impression of clumsiness that harbor seals exhibit on land is quickly changed to one of exquisite grace under water.

Much larger and less common than harbor seals are elephant seals, the largest of all pinnipeds. The species of elephant seal that occurs in Puget Sound is the northern elephant seal. It breeds and pups on islands from Central to Baja California and migrates over much of the eastern North Pacific Ocean on feeding forays.

These seals rarely haul out while on migration, hence they are not likely to be seen or recognized in the Puget Sound area. When they are sighted, it is usually on a day when the water is flat and calm. A resting elephant seal, drifting with the tide, looks like a low nun buoy or the tip of a submerged deadhead log. But suddenly it disappears! With patience and luck, one may see it reappear about 20 minutes later, bobbing to the surface as it raises its ungainly nose to the air to breathe and look around before taking a short nap. Although the seal remains alert to approaching motorboats and other disturbances, it often closes its eyes. Indian hunters took advantage of napping ele-

phant seals by quietly paddling close to them and harpooning them. The elephant seals' thick blubber was valued as a condiment and as a source of cooking oil.

There is a pronounced sexual dimorphism in elephant seals; males are several times larger than females and possess a floppy proboscis which hangs over the upper lip like a stocking cap or a shortened elephant's trunk, hence the common name. The pelt is silvery gray immediately after molt, then turns tan or brown. The molt occurs in winter and spring and is unusual in that the entire layer of epidermis is shed with the hair. The seals remain hauled out on land for about a month until the molt is complete. After long months at sea, the pelt may acquire greenish or reddish patches of algae and some seals even have barnacles growing on their toes.

Breeding and pupping season lasts from December to February, during which time the otherwise fraternizing bulls defend areas of beach from one another and establish what is known as a dominance hierarchy. The most dominant—or "alpha"—bulls control the prime areas of beach where the females gather to give birth and nurse their pups. Alpha bulls don't pay much attention to the pups or even to the females until the last week of nursing, when the females ovulate and breeding activities begin again.

Alpha bulls become enraged if another male intrudes on their territory. The alpha bull—the "harem-master"—rumbles across the beach like a flesh-covered tank, bearing down on his adversary with a decidedly evil-eyed look. As the harem bull nears the intruder he stops, blows his nose, rears back, and lets out a hearty belching threat, which resonates in his floppy nostrils. This is usually enough to frighten away most interlopers but if it is not, the two rivals plant themselves chest to chest and slash at each other's necks with their dagger-like canine teeth. Meanwhile, seemingly oblivious to the stakes of the battle, the females bleat and sneeze in the background and cool off by throwing sand and pebbles upon their backs. The alpha bull almost always wins these conflicts, usually because he is larger and a more experienced fighter. If he does not win, he is no longer harem master.

*A curious harbor seal in a kelp bed*

# Harbor Seal
## *Phoca vitulina*

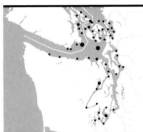

Length 1.2–1.8 m (3.9–5.9 ft)
Weight 45–105 kg (99–231 lbs)

**Status and Distribution** Harbor seals are year-round residents in Puget Sound and are relatively abundant on haulout areas at low tide and on breeding rookeries.

The entire harbor seal population in the state of Washington is estimated to be 7,000 seals. Some seals move between the inshore and coastal waters of both Washington and British Columbia. A 1977-78 census counted about 2,600 seals in the entire Puget Sound area (Everitt et al., 1978). In southern Puget Sound, 340 seals were counted, mostly around or on Gertrude Island, which has remained isolated from the general public because of its proximity to the McNeil Island federal penitentiary. In Hood Canal, there were 730 seals; in northern Puget Sound, the Strait of Juan de Fuca, and among the isolated islets and reefs of the San Juan Archipelago, 1,500 seals.

In the early 1940s, the state population of harbor seals was estimated to be 6,000 to 10,000 (Scheffer and Slipp, 1948). Because it was believed harbor seals ate significant amounts of commercially valuable fishes, primarily salmon, a bounty was placed on them. From 1947 to 1960, an estimated 17,000 seals were killed, with no apparent enhancement of commercial fisheries resulting. Harbor seals and all other marine mammals are now protected from harassment or killing by federal law.

**Food and Critical Habitat** A study of the food habits of harbor seals indicates that the harbor seals in greater Puget Sound primarily eat species of fish that are not commercially valuable or even palatable to most humans (Calambokidis et al., 1978). Half of the identifiable bones in fecal remains of northern Puget Sound harbor seals were of blackbelly eelpout; more than half of those from Hood Canal were of Pacific hake; and more than half of those from southern Puget Sound were of the Pacific staghorn sculpin. Scatological studies may under-represent the actual amount of larger fish eaten, however, because the larger bones may not be consumed and passed for biologists to gather and examine.

In a study of seal diets conducted in Puget Sound between December 1927 and August 1930 (Scheffer and Sperry, 1931), stomach contents were examined that did include fleshy remains. In citing this study, Keyes (1968) notes: "The general distribution of food by volume was 93.6 percent, fish; 5.8 percent, molluscs; and 0.6 percent, crustaceans. The chief species of fish, in order of frequency of occurrence, were flounders, Pacific herring, tomcod, hake, sculpins, pollock, shiner perch, cod, and rockfish. Salmon were found in two stomachs. Squids were eaten in winter and octopi were eaten in summer." Such studies seem to indicate that the damaging effect of harbor seals on the salmon fishery may have been exaggerated. This is of little consolation, however, to a fisherman who has just had a valuable fish damaged or "stolen" from him by a hungry harbor seal.

Harbor seals can dive to 90 m (295 ft) and remain underwater for more than 20 minutes. Typically, a harbor seal foraging for prey remains submerged for three to five minutes and then bobs to the surface for a 30-second breather and to look around. At low tide they are generally found hauled out to digest the food caught during the previous tidal movement.

Harbor seals are very shy and rarely allow people or boats to approach a haulout area before they abandon it by rolling, falling, or scrambling into the water, where they are better equipped to protect themselves. Because of their shyness, rookeries and haulout areas require protection from human disturbance and development.

# Elephant Seal
## *Mirounga angustirostris*

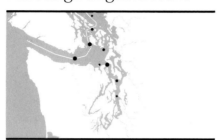

| Length | Males | 5 m (16.4 ft) |
|--------|---------|------------------|
|        | Females | 3 m (9.8 ft) |
| Weight | Males | 2,000 kg (4,400 lbs) |
|        | Females | 800 kg (1,760 lbs) |

**Status and Distribution** The northern elephant seal is an occasional visitor to Puget Sound and a regular inhabitant of the eastern North Pacific Ocean. A few solitary individuals come into this area each spring after the main population has dispersed from the breeding and pupping islands along the coast of California and Mexico to feed over much of the North Pacific. Even fewer come into the area in the fall as they return to their breeding range. Most of the visitors are males, which forage farther north than females.

The entire population of northern elephant seals was nearly exterminated in the mid-1880s by commercial sealers, who decimated breeding populations numbering in the tens of thousands, including females with pups. For the first half of this century there was little likelihood of seeing an elephant seal anywhere except near breeding islands. The North Pacific population has since recovered and is estimated to be 30,000 seals reoccupying much of their former range. However, because probably fewer than 100 elephant seals remained after the slaughter of the 1800s they are now all inbred and have lost forever the genetic resilience that millions of years of evolution had given them. An epidemic of some organism new to elephant seals could spread rapidly through the population if they were by chance homogeneously unresistant to it.

**Food and Critical Habit** The food of elephant seals varies with the area in which they are foraging, but in inshore habitats it primarily consists of benthic or bottom-dwelling species. The stomach contents of a seal chased ashore by killer whales on the west coast of Vancouver Island contained Pacific hagfish eggs and remains. Others taken at sea contained ratfish, dogfish, skates, and squids.

Elephant seals are deep divers, but little information exists about how deep they can go, except to estimate the depth at which prey might have been caught. Three young elephant seals were accidentally caught on hook and line at 183 m (600 ft), and adults can presumably go much deeper than that. The length of a typical foraging dive is about 20 minutes, and the maximum recorded dive is 40 minutes.

# Sea Lions
## *Otariidae*

On very calm days near Race Rocks off Victoria, British Columbia, one can sometimes hear a raucous barking and roaring that is audible for miles. The source of this racket is California sea lions, which bark like circus "seals," and northern sea lions, which roar like lions, hauled out together on the rocks. These are the two species of otarriid seals that are found in Puget Sound. Otariids are called "eared" seals, because of the very small, rolled-up external pinnnae just behind their eyes. They differ from the true seals by virtue of their hind flippers, which they can rotate forward in order to walk on all fours. When they swim, they stroke with their leathery, paddle-shaped foreflippers and use their hindflippers like a rudder.

The larger and more common of the two "eared" seals found in Puget Sound is the northern sea lion. Both sexes of this species have tawny colored pelts which appear almost white when wet, and the male develops a thick yellow mane that surrounds its disproportionately huge neck.

Male sea lions grow much larger than females. The size dimorphism in many species of pinnipeds is attributed to their polygynous breeding habits. Males fight viciously with one another to attain and defend their harems, which may number up to 100 females. Both sexes are sexually mature when they are five-years old, but young males are not large enough or strong enough to defend breeding territory until about seven or eight years of age. As the young males grow larger and stronger, they are better able to defend a larger territory and thereby mate with more females.

The smaller and less common sea lion in greater Puget Sound is the California sea lion, whose pelt is brown, turning to very dark brown when it is wet. Their color makes California sea lions easily distinguishable from northern sea lions in the water, where size is difficult to estimate. On land, California sea lions can be distinguished from northern sea lions because they are smaller and darker and there is a prominent crest on the males' heads.

California sea lions occupy a feeding niche similar to that of northern sea lions. They haul out together in some places, but their evolutionary paths have taken them in opposite directions to breed. California sea lions breed off California and Mexico and are the most abundant sea lion south of Puget Sound. Northern sea lions breed in Alaska and British Columbia and are most abundant north of Puget Sound.

*Male California sea lion (lower left) with females.*
*A northern sea lion (right)*

# Northern or Steller's Sea Lion
## *Eumetopias jubatus*

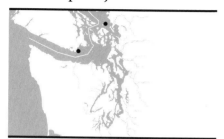

| Length | Males | 3 m (9.8 ft) |
|---|---|---|
| | Females | 2 m (6.6 ft) |
| Weight | Males | 1,000 kg (2,200 lbs) |
| | Females | 300 kg (660 lbs) |

**Status and Distribution** The northern sea lion population numbers about 300,000 animals, most of which are in the northern extent of a range extending from Southern California to Alaska and the Sea of Okhotsk. Breeding and pupping occur on coastal islands along this range from mid-May to mid-July, when virtually the entire population aggregates near the breeding islands and few venture into inland waters.

Northern sea lions move into Puget Sound in the fall, and by midwinter they may number several hundred in the area. They forage throughout the inland waters, but their favorite haulout areas are in northern Puget Sound at Race Rocks, Sombrio Point, and Sucia Island. A 1978 survey at these locations showed a peak population of 259 sea lions in April and none in the area in June, July, and August (Everitt et al., 1979).

**Food and Critical Habitat** Northern sea lions are opportunistic feeders. In Puget Sound they eat locally abundant fish species—rockfish, skate, hake, salmon, halibut, black cod—as well as squid and octopus (Pike, 1958). In some areas sea lions have incurred the wrath of commercial fishermen for the damage they have wrought to fishing gear and fisheries. Occasionally, bullet-ridden carcasses of this species float to Pacific Northwest beaches. Individual sea lions learn the hard way where or where not to forage, but they have little choice about where to haul out. Major haulout areas are used year after year and are critical habitat for the species.

# California Sea Lion
## *Zalophus californianus*

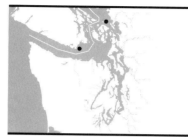

| Length | Males | 2 m (6.6 ft) |
|---|---|---|
| | Females | 1.8 m (5.9 ft) |
| Weight | Males | 270 kg (594 lbs) |
| | Females | 90 kg (198 lbs) |

**Status and Distribution** California sea lions roam farther afield during their migration than northern sea lions. They breed on islands off California and Mexico during May and June, then some males migrate north as far as British Columbia for the winter. A few of these young and adult male sea lions show up in Puget Sound in December, which is the peak month of their occurrence in the area, and they may be found as late as May. The highest single count of this species was 75 animals hauled out at Race Rocks and Sombrio Point in December 1977 (Everitt et al., 1979).

The total population of California sea lions in the eastern North Pacific was 100,000 to 125,000 in the late 1970s. Most of these animals haul out on remote islands off Southern California and Baja California.

**Food and Critical Habitat** California sea lions are opportunistic feeders on locally abundant fish species and cephalopods. They seem to prefer the latter, judging from stomach contents of sea lions that have been collected (Keyes, 1968). In Oregon and California they cause some damage to salmon fisheries, but in Puget Sound they usually leave the area before the major runs of salmon arrive.

The critical habitats for California sea lions in this region are the haulout areas where they rest between forages.

# Rorquals
## *Balaenopteridae*

Whales are classified according to their feeding habits and the ones that have adapted the most specialized feeding strategy are the members of the family Balaenopteridae. These giants "gulp" large numbers of small fishes or swarms of invertebrates in one mouthful. The entire throat area is composed of longitudinal pleats of skin and blubber which permit great distention to encompass their prey.

These species of whales range in size from about 9 m (29.5 ft) to 30 m (100 ft) long. The smallest of the rorquals is the minke whale. It is black on its back, with a beautiful pattern of steel-gray streaks near the tail and on the back behind the blow hole. Most minke whales have a dark cloud-gray patch on the side of the chest. The whale's snout or rostrum is very pointed and has a ridge that runs down the middle to the blow hole. It has small flippers and a distinctive shoulder band of white, which can be seen under water at close range.

The Makah Indians regularly hunted minke whales near Cape Flattery for their prized meat and oil, but the American whalers found them much too shy and difficult to catch. Until recently minke whales have been spared heavy commercial whaling pressure. However, in the past ten years, as commercial catches of larger whales have dwindled, whalers have begun to harvest this smallest species of Balaenopteridae. In coastal areas where they are hunted commercially, minke whale populations are quickly depleted. The eastern North Pacific stocks have so far been spared this harvest and could therefore be useful for comparative studies with exploited stocks.

The largest of the rorqual whales likely to be found in Puget Sound is the humpback whale. Prior to the 20th century, this species was the most common large rorqual in coastal and inland marine waters of all oceans. But its coastal and inshore habits proved too convenient for whalers, and it was nearly exterminated throughout its range before it was protected from commercial whaling worldwide in 1966 by the International Whaling Commission. At least 20,000 of these leviathans were killed in the eastern North Pacific in the 20th century alone. They are now scarce in almost all of their former habitats.

Humpbacks are easy to identify because they raise their backs in a prominant hump when they dive, and they often splash their flippers and flukes in apparent play. They can be identified individually by characteristic marks and pigmentation patterns on the fin, flippers, and flukes. Humpbacks are pigmented black, with varying amounts of white on the belly. They have extremely long flippers, approximately one-third the body length, several rows of knobby bumps on the head, and a small irregularly shaped dorsal fin on the back.

Humpbacks are frolicsome and gregarious whales. They are especially fun to watch because they sometimes exhibit great curiosity about people and boats, especially in their tropical breeding grounds. They travel in groups, communicating with one another by making low mooing and chirping sounds, which travel long distances underwater.

During breeding season humpback whale sounds are patterned into songs, which are repeated sequences of sounds. Interestingly, all singers of a population seem to sing the same "hit" song during a given year, but their songs appear to change from year to year. These songs are very beautiful to hear and have proven quite popular with human audiences. Several phonograph records of them have been produced, and a recording of one song of a humpback was launched into space on the Voyager I flight, man's first message bottle cast into the cosmic sea. Perhaps at last humans are developing an appreciation of these marvelous creatures for more than the meat and products they have to offer.

Minke and humpback whales are the only rorquals likely to occur in Puget Sound and are the only ones discussed in the species descriptions. However, among the other members of this family are two species—the fin whale and the giant blue whale—which deserve mention because they are potential visitors to this area.

The fin whale (*Balaenoptera physalus*) is the second largest whale on earth. Its normal range includes the coastal waters of the Pacific Northwest, and occasionally one of these behemoths enters the inshore waters in pursuit of shoals of herring. Because fin whales have been severely overexploited in past decades throughout their range, they are rarely seen in the eastern North Pacific Ocean or in inland waters. The exception is Prince William Sound, Alaska, where a few fin whales feed during the summer. Before fin whale populations were overharvested by whalers, there were occasional fin whales sightings in Puget Sound. These waters are still potential feeding habitat for fin whales, and if the stocks recover it is possible that they might occur here again someday.

The blue whale (*Balaenoptera musculus*) is the largest of all animals that have ever inhabited the

*Minke whale about to envelop
a shoal of herring*

earth. Its great size was not to its advantage however when man the hunter appeared on the scene. A blue whale that entered coastal waters to forage was considered the ultimate prize by whalers. Although they were too big and powerful for most primitive whalers, a few daring souls—including Makah whalers—were able to land one occasionally. Then, toward the end of the 19th century, harpoon cannons, rockets, and motor-powered vessels were employed by whalers and the hunt for the blue whale became deadly efficient.

The *coup de grace* for the blue whale was delivered by the development in the 1920s of offshore, pelagic, whale factory ships, which extended the hunt from coastal waters to the open seas. From that time on, the decimation of the blue whale was methodical and thorough wherever they were found. In the early 1930s, as many as 30,000 blue whales were killed per year, mostly in waters around Antarctica. In 1966, blue whales finally received worldwide protection from commercial whaling by the International Whaling Commission.

We can take heart that a small population of blue whales is known to still inhabit the eastern North Pacific Ocean, and at least one juvenile blue whale has visited Puget Sound in modern times (Scheffer and Slipp, 1948). Anyone lucky enough to see this pale blue colossus the size of a boxcar, with its spout rising 20 to 30 feet in the air, will unquestionably be humbled by the experience. Perhaps this species will survive and once again the sea will be "marked with their huge forms and towering spouts" as Captain Charles Scammon (1874), a famous whaling captain, found them over 100 years ago.

# Minke Whale
## *Balaenoptera acutorostrata*

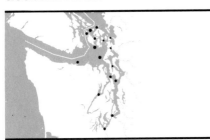

Length to 9 m (29.5 ft)
Weight to 9 metric tons (9.9 tons)

**Status and Distribution** Minke whales can regularly be seen in the eastern Strait of Juan of Fuca and around the San Juan Archipelago. They also can be seen in Admiralty Inlet, Hood Canal, Possession Sound, and in southern Puget Sound as far as the Nisqually Delta when herring are abundant.

Some minke whales are distinctively marked or scarred and can be recognized individually. They have been observed often enough in particular locations to suggest that at least some are residents of the area. Around the San Juan Islands, there are probably no more than 20 of these regularly occurring whales.

In the late summer and fall the local population appears to increase. Judging from the small size of many of the minke whales seen around Hein Bank, Salmon Bank, and Partridge Bank in the fall, the increase may be largely juveniles. It is not known if they are offspring of resident whales or are visitors passing through. Long-term observation of recognizable whales in the area could answer that question and provide important information on the life history of minke whales.

**Food and Critical Habitat** Minke whales feed upon herring and other small schooling fishes in coastal and inshore waters, and in other areas where these food species gather in abundance. Minke whales are very quiet and unobtrusive, but as they surface to feed—mouth agape—they often stir up flocks of gulls and other seabirds that are dining on the same prey. The pandemonium that results betrays the whale's presence on the feeding grounds. During daytime, minke whales are almost always feeding or travelling somewhere to feed, and they pay little attention to boats, except to avoid them.

Feeding areas vary with the seasons, and even with the tides. However, since habitat for the prey is ultimately essential to the predator, the spawning areas of little schooling fishes can be considered critical for the continued survival of minke whales.

*Humpback whale*

# Humpback Whale
## *Megaptera novaeangliae*

Length to 16 m (52.4 ft)
Weight to 40 metric tons (44 tons)

**Status and Distribution** Humpbacks are found worldwide, but they are considered endangered throughout their range due to overexploitation. They occur only rarely in Puget Sound at present, although historically they were so common that shore whaling stations were established at Victoria, British Columbia, the Strait of Georgia (Schmitt et al., 1980), and along the outer coast of British Columbia and Washington State. In recent years there have been occasional reports of small groups of humpback whales in the area, and they regularly occur during fall in the coastal waters of Washington off the Olympic Peninsula.

The number of humpbacks in the entire eastern North Pacific is estimated to be 1,500 animals migrating between summer feeding grounds in Alaska and winter breeding grounds in Hawaii and Mexico. Some have been seen in the Puget Sound region in recent years and the prognosis is favorable that more will be seen if there is suitable habitat for them. Because humpback whales are individually identifiable, it is possible to determine which individual whales consistently return to the area and where else they go, especially during breeding and calving season.

**Food and Critical Habitat** Humpback whales are euryphagous; they feed on a variety of species of small schooling fishes and invertebrates. They can eat some relatively large species such as cod and squid, but they seem to prefer herring and euphausiids if available. It was probably the great blooms of herring in Puget Sound waters which attracted humpback whales here in the past, and it will be a similar factor which will attract them here in the future.

As with minke whales, the ephemeral nature of food abundance and its location according to seasons and tides makes it impossible to precisely say what locations constitute critical feeding habitat for humpback whales. Such determinations depend upon what is considered critical habitat for the prey. Potential feeding habitats exist in coastal and inland marine waters from California to Alaska. It may be that humpback whale populations are currently well below the carrying capacity of these habitats, and the whales select areas in which it is easiest or most efficient to feed. Or perhaps they select areas with less nuisance from people or predators. The National Marine Fisheries Service of the National Oceanic and Atmospheric Administration has initiated research to determine whether food supply or interference most affects the distribution of humpback whales in selected habitats. This research is crucial to attempts to adequately protect this endangered species.

# Gray Whales
## *Eschrichtiidae*

The simplest feeding method among baleen whales has been developed by the gray whales, which "grub" their prey from bottom sediments in shallow water. It is not difficult to imagine that this habit might have been utilized by the earliest baleen whales, since prey is abundant in the shallow mud substrate, it is close to shore, and it cannot escape. The feeding method seems to be as follows: the whale rolls on its side with its head parallel to the bottom, then, pumping its tongue like a syringe, squirts water out of the side of its mouth to stir up the mud. With an inward stroke of the tongue, water, mud, and benthic organisms are sucked into the whale's mouth; with an outward stroke, the mud and water are forced back out, leaving prey tangled in the baleen. Then, with a slight smacking of its lips, the whale sluices its meal down its gullet.

A captive gray whale in San Diego named 'Gigi' showed observers how efficiently this system operated, and helped scientists understand how the whale could extract benthic organisms from mud without having to shovel the substrate with its tender lips and snout (Ray and Schevill, 1974). The facial skin of these whales is unscathed, but the baleen shows wear from filtering rocks and grit. The wear is usually on the left side, indicating that whales may preferentially roll that side down.

Gray whales can be easily recognized by their gray color and the lack of a dorsal fin. A series of ridges or bumps along the back creates a reptilian or sea serpent appearance for those who see them for the first time. The snout is slightly arched on top and looks bluntly wedge-shaped viewed from above. It is always studded with patches of small white barnacles that are surrounded by yellowish orange swarms of whale lice (*Cyamus* sp.). There are 140 to 180 creamy white baleen plates on each side of the upper jaw.

There is good reason to elaborate on facial descriptions, because this is one whale "face" that whale watchers may get to see. Gray whales have a curious behavioral trait, manifested by a maneuver known as "spyhopping," in which they raise their heads vertically out of the water to about eye level and remain that way for a few seconds. They spyhop frequently while feeding, and may even poke their heads startlingly close to small boats that happen to be in the vicinity. Whether they are really looking around seems to depend on the eye being out of the water, and often it is not.

The sight of a whale at close range can evoke a mixture of awe and terror to the uninitiated observer. There is no reason to fear, however, because gray whales are not known to be easily provoked. Gray whales are even-tempered and even friendly unless attacked, at which times they can live up to their nickname "devilfish," given them by early whalers whose small boats were soundly thrashed by flailing flukes. There is reason for caution, however, when whale watching from a small boat. Gray whales are unpredictable, and one may "breach" unexpectedly, leaping out of the water and creating a thunderous splash as it falls. A small boat could get rocked around and inundated by these antics.

Near breeding lagoons there is a lot of breaching and other spectacular behavior, but around Puget Sound they usually just stir up mud and spyhop occasionally. Nonetheless, they are fun to watch and it is wonderful to have them visit each summer. Gray whales have become tourist attractions at many coastal points where they pass on their migrations, and tour boats visit their breeding lagoons each winter. There is some concern that this increased interest in whale watching constitutes harassment which will drive them from their habitats and to eventual extinction, but this is unlikely. Concern for their welfare is better directed toward maintaining their habitats free of pollutants, which are deposited in the substrate and work their way insidiously into the food chain.

# California Gray Whale
*Eschrichtius robustus*

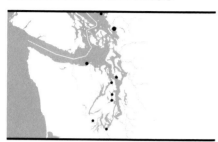

Length    males to 13 m (42.6 ft)
          females to 14 m (46.2 ft)
Weight to 30 metric tons (33 tons)

**Status and Distribution**   Gray whales are only known to occur in the eastern North Pacific Ocean and adjacent seas and inland waters, but they formerly occurred in the Atlantic Ocean as well. They are listed as endangered under United States law, but it is generally agreed that the eastern North Pacific population has recovered to near pre exploitation levels, estimated at 15,647 animals in 1980 (Reilly, 1981).

The gray whale is considered a sustained management stock by the International Whaling Commission, which means a commercial quota (about 300) may be taken each year. Some are taken commercially by the Soviets in the Bering Sea, and some are taken for subsistence purposes by Eskimos in the Bering and Chuckchi Seas.

This species conducts the longest and most regular migration known for any mammal: from the ice-strewn feeding grounds of the Bering and Chuckchi Seas in summer to the warm, protected calving and breeding lagoons off Baja California in winter. For much of their long migration they follow the beaches, promontories, and coastlines along the way. A few come into Puget Sound each year as the main procession of the population passes along the outer coast heading south in November and December and north from April to June. A few hangers-on are occasionally found in the area at other times of the year.

**Food and Critical Habitat**   The most prevalent food species of gray whales are amphipods, which are found in incredible abundance in the Bering Sea, and bottom-dwelling or bottom-spawning species such as rainbow smelt. In Puget Sound, gray whales forage in backwaters and bays for a variety of invertebrates, mysids, fish larvae, and small schooling fishes.

Critical habitats for grubbing are shallow mud-bottom bays that are one to three whale body lengths (up to 40 m) deep, such as Bellingham Bay and the southern reaches of Puget Sound.

While feeding, gray whales breathe irregularly, but average one respiration for each minute submerged and usually do not stay below for more than a few minutes before surfacing for air. They can stay submerged for 20 minutes or more, and can sneak a breath without being seen if they are being pursued.

# Toothed Whales and Dolphins
## *Delphinidae*

There are more species in the family Delphinidae than in any other family of Cetacea. The common denominator of these species is that they all possess numerous conical teeth in their upper and lower jaws, which are used for grasping prey. They range in length from about 2 to 9 m (6.5 to 29.5 ft). The smaller delphinids are called dolphins, and the larger ones—longer than 4 m (13 ft)—are usually called whales.

Some delphinids, such as the killer whale, are found nearly worldwide, while others have evolved to fill particular geographic niches. Because Puget Sound's inshore waters open to the vast North Pacific Ocean, a multitude of species whose distribution may be largely dictated by the abundance of prey and by the dynamic processes of currents and climate may wander into these waters. When squids are abundant in the Strait of Juan de Fuca, for example, those species that are teuthophagous—squid eaters—may be found here. Unusually cold or warm water off shore of the Strait may attract certain species that are normally found in colder or warmer waters.

Many species of delphinids are likely to occur in or near greater Puget Sound, but the resident and regularly occurring species are killer whales, Pacific white-sided dolphins, pilot whales, and Risso's dolphin. The most visible and charismatic of these is the killer whale, also known as orca or blackfish.

The largest of the delphinids, the killer whale is a strikingly beautiful creature. It has a glossy black back, a brilliant white-patterned belly, a white oval patch over each eye, a sweep of white on its flanks, and a variable saddle of gray behind its dorsal fin. It is the male killer whale's impressive dorsal fin that makes it such a familiar sight in Puget Sound. This large triangular fin may grow to 130 cm (6 ft) in height and 90 cm (3 ft) long at the base on an adult male. The female's dorsal fin is somewhat smaller; about 60 cm (2 ft) in height and length.

Killer whales travel in family groups called pods. These pods establish relatively local year-round territory, rather than migrating extremely long distances from feeding areas to breeding grounds. Calves remain with the pod into which they are born long after weaning and may remain for life. This particular aspect of social structure is being studied in the killer whale pods of Puget Sound because of the implication of genetic isolation and its bearing on the survival of the local population. The genetic identity of local populations here and elsewhere may be ascertained from studies of tissues or blood samples—thereby offering an unprecedented opportunity for whale stock assessment. Genetic isolation implies that a depleted local stock may not be revitalized by an adjacent stock, but it may be entirely replaced if the habitat remains suitable and available.

A fascinating aspect of killer whale behavior is the remarkable sounds they make—screams, clicks, and whistles—to communicate with one another and to locate prey. There is increasing evidence that these sounds enable the whales to communicate over distances of several miles. Thus, individual members of a pod may forage far beyond each other's visual horizon yet maintain finely coordinated group movements while herding a school of fish. There is also evidence that populations of killer whales from different geographic regions have distinct repertoires of sounds, called dialects. Scientists are investigating these sounds to ascertain their role in the communication between members of the species and for their potential role in interspecific communication. It may be possible someday to communicate at length with these intelligent creatures. In the meantime, we have much to patiently learn about them in the wild, and there is no better place to do that than in Puget Sound.

Another characteristic delphinid in the Puget Sound region is the Pacific white-sided dolphin. A beautiful and playful creature, this dolphin may be seen frolicking in the bow wave of vessels underway and leaping full length out of the water alongside the boat. It has a black back with a pair of hourglass-shaped streaks running from the forehead up over the back and down along the flank to the tail. The shoulder region and belly are extensively white, and the rear half of the large sickle-shaped dorsal fin is light gray.

These dolphins are gregarious animals and travel in schools that may number into the hundreds in coastal waters, although it is usually smaller groups that venture inshore. This species also uses sound to communicate and locate prey. Its clicking sounds are actually echo-location signals so sophisticated that these dolphins can discriminate differences in size and texture of sound reflecting objects. Using these sounds, dolphins can avoid fixed obstacles and even the fine mesh of fishing nets as they pursue their prey at depths and over distances where vision is useless.

Pilot whales are almost entirely black but have an indistinct grayish saddle behind the dorsal fin and a thin anchor-shaped white patch on their bellies. The forehead of the pilot whale is very bulbous, extending forward to the mouth, and it pushes a prominent bow wave ahead of the whale as it surfaces to breathe. The disproportionately large dorsal fin is located very far forward on the body and in males is sufficiently flexible to often hook backwards.

Pilot whales are gregarious animals that display affection and concern for others of their species. These behavioral patterns have been exploited in many parts of the world by fishermen who have driven them ashore like cattle and slaughtered entire schools of pilot whales for their meat and oil. Hundreds and even thousands of these whales can be taken at one time in this way, often to the detriment of a local population or stock.

Sometimes schools of pilot whales strand themselves en masse, and there is much controversy concerning the reason for this suicidal behavior. Whatever the reason, these mass strandings have occurred among pilot whales and a few other gregarious species for eons, as evidenced by the fossil record, and does not necessarily imply man's destruction of the ocean habitat. There have been no mass strandings of pilot whales recorded in Washington State, but several individual strandings have occurred here.

Another dolphin that is relatively common off the coast of Washington and episodically comes inshore is Risso's dolphin. Sometimes a school of a dozen or so of these dolphins will hitch a ride on the bow of a vessel underway; at other times they will entirely avoid approach. Their coloring is dark gray with extensive splotches and scratches of white on the head and back. The forehead is blunt with a peculiar longitudinal crease running down the middle, and they have a large curved dorsal fin.

Another species which has occurred here but is a rare and unlikely visitor is the false killer whale. It looks superficially like a pilot whale and is about the same size, but has a wedge-shaped forehead. It is black, with a dorsal fin about midlength along its back. The most recent documented occurrence of a false killer whale in this area was in May 1937 when one was shot and killed in southern Puget Sound (Scheffer and Slipp, 1948). The species accounts that follow are only for those species that occur regularly in Puget Sound.

*A breaching male orca*

# Killer Whale
## *Orcinus orca*

| Length | males | to 9.1 m (30 ft) |
|--------|-------|------------------|
|        | females | to 8.2 m (27 ft) |
| Weight | males | 4.5 metric tons (5 tons) |
|        | females | 2.7 metric tons (3 tons) |

**Status and Distribution** Killer whales are found worldwide, especially in productive coastal waters. In the eastern North Pacific Ocean they occur from the Equator to Alaska, and are relatively abundant in the Pacific Northwest. They range throughout these inland waters where the water is deep enough to permit their passage. Historically, they have even swum into the mouths of rivers. such as the Duwamish, Nisqually, and Fraser; and they were occasionally caught in fish traps before the traps were outlawed in the 1930s.

There are three resident pods totaling about 80 killer whales that regularly forage in the waters of Puget Sound, the Washington coast, and off British Columbia. Several other "transient" pods totalling less than two dozen whales come into the area from time to time but they never stay long (Bigg et al., 1976).

A detailed inventory of whales in the three resident pods— designated J, K, and L—showed that as of summer 1980, J pod contained eight adult females, three adult males, and eight juvenile whales from one to eight years of age. The K and L pods frequently travelled together and subdivided into smaller groups which collectively contained 30 adult females, 12 adult males, and 20 juveniles of undetermined age (Balcomb et al., 1980).

The local population of killer whales was "cropped" in the 1960s and 1970s, when many of them were captured for live display in oceanaria. During this period the population was reduced from more than 100 to 68 in 1976 (Bigg and Wolman, 1975; Balcomb and Goebel, 1976). From 1976 to 1980, the remaining population has increased at a rate of about two whales per year.

**Food and Critical Habitat** Killer whales are so named because they can kill and eat virtually any creature in the sea, and in some areas their predation on other marine mammals can be particularly bloody and seemingly cruel. In some parts of their worldwide range their diet consists largely of herring, while in others it may be primarily sharks, marine mammals, or squids. In Puget Sound, killer whales eat fish— salmon, rockfish, cod, and other available species. They usually do not bother the other marine mammals in this area, nor do they pose a threat to boaters or divers. Puget Sound's resident killer whales seem adapted to human presence and rather effectively and casually avoid the occasional person who tries to get in their way.

Because killer whales are top carnivores in the marine ecosystem, the entire Puget Sound habitat is critical, especially those areas where there are bountiful runs of salmon. Wherever salmon are abundant in these inland marine waters, killer whales probably can be found. The Indian fishermen who were here when white men arrived had a simple summary of this relationship: "no blackfish, no fish." To conserve this habitat for whales, we must protect the entire Sound and its freshwater spawning streams from contamination and pollution. And, we must wisely control harvesting to assure the survival of salmon and other living resources.

# Pacific White-sided Dolphin
## *Lagenorhynchus obliquidens*

Length to 2.2 m (7.2 ft)
Weight to 90 kg (198 lbs)

**Status and Distribution** The North Pacific population of white-sided dolphins is estimated to be 30,000 to 50,000 off Japan, and at least that many in the eastern North Pacific. The population is distributed mostly along the continental shelf, from Baja California to the Gulf of Alaska and from Korea to the Kuril Islands, with a slight seasonal shift to the south in winter and to the north in summer. Sometimes a passing vessel may be in nearly constant company of small groups of these dolphins. White-sided dolphins have been seen in schools numbering more than a thousand and they frequently aggregate with other cetacean species to feed.

During summer and early fall, schools of up to a hundred of these beautiful dolphins enter the Strait of Juan de Fuca and forage as far inshore as Port Angeles, but only rarely do they venture farther east. There are a few sightings of these dolphins as far as Haro Strait and Rosario Strait around the San Juan Archipelago, and one specimen was collected off Victoria (Scheffer and Slipp, 1948).

**Food and Critical Habitat** Pacific white-sided dolphins feed primarily on squids, which usually occur with increased summer incursions of oceanic water into the Strait of Juan de Fuca.

# Short-finned Pilot Whale
## *Globicephala macrorhynchus*

| Length | males | to 6.9 m (22.6 ft) |
|--------|-------|--------------------|
|        | females | to 5 m (16.4 ft) |
| Weight | males | to 1,200 kg (2,640 lbs) |
|        | females | to 800 kg (1,760 lbs) |

**Status and Distribution** Short-finned pilot whales are found in tropical latitudes of the Atlantic and Indian Oceans and in the Pacific Ocean from the Gulf of Alaska and Japan to Peru and Australia. The North Pacific population alone numbers hundreds of thousands. In the summer months schools of a few to many hundreds of pilot whales are common near the escarpments and sea canyons off the entrance to the Strait of Juan de Fuca. During this time some of these small whales may enter the Strait of Juan de Fuca, and they have been reported as far inshore as Hein Bank, off San Juan Island.

**Food and Critical Habitat** Pilot whales are deep divers that feed on squids, which are found near oceanic convergences, upwelling areas, and along the continental shelf, especially where there are sharp changes in bottom topography. The inshore waters of the Strait of Juan de Fuca offer temporary feeding habitat only when squids are present in summer and fall.

# Risso's Dolphin
## *Grampus griseus*

Length 3.6 m (11.8 ft)
Weight 1,984 kg (900 lbs)

**Status and Distribution** Risso's dolphins are distributed according to the vagaries of oceanographic conditions in tropical and temporate latitudes of all oceans. They are relatively common off the northern coast of Washington and occasionally come inshore. The most recent record of this species in Puget Sound is a single stranding near Port Townsend in March 1975 (Everitt et al., 1979).

**Food and Critical Habitat** This species is teuthophagous, or squid-eating, and is often found in association with other squid-eating species that seem to spend their entire lifetime searching the current interfaces and upwelling zones of the ocean in search of their prey.

*White-sided dolphins*

# Porpoises
## *Phocoenidae*

Porpoises are often confused with dolphins because laymen, fishermen, and even scientists usually don't discriminate between the names "porpoise" and "dolphin." The members of these two families can be identified by their teeth: porpoises have spade-shaped teeth, and dolphins have conical teeth. In the eastern North Pacific there are only two species of porpoise, the harbor porpoise and Dall's porpoise, both of which are found regularly in Puget Sound.

The harbor porpoise is the smallest and most inconspicuous resident cetacean in Puget Sound. Historically, harbor porpoises were common throughout the inland waters of the Pacific Northwest and they were taken for food by Northwest Indians. They were caught occasionally in salmon traps, or more frequently were speared by hunters in canoes. These little cetaceans are extremely shy of boats, so capturing them required great skill and patience. It is virtually impossible to approach one closely with a power boat, and they never play in the bow wave of vessels.

Because harbor porpoises are so shy, it is difficult to get close to one in the wild. It usually looks like an automobile tire rolling slowly and bobbing at the water's surface—that is, until a triangular dorsal fin appears at top of the roll. However, a stranded harbor porpoise can be positively identified by its little spade-shaped teeth (about 22 in both upper and lower jaws) and its striking pigmentation. Harbor porpoises are gray to black on their backs, shading to white on the belly. They have dark gray flippers and a dark gray stripe leading from the gape of the mouth to the leading edge of the flipper. During breeding season (late summer and fall in Puget Sound), the pigmentation of mature males sharpens in definition and a prominent silver gray "helmet" emerges on the forehead, strikingly set against its dark back.

Dall's porpoises are larger and much more conspicuous than harbor porpoises. They swim at speeds up to 30 knots and send up little roostertails of spray every time they surface to take a breath. In contrast to the harbor porpoise, Dall's porpoises don't shy away from humans. In fact, they seem to love to ride the bow wave of vessels, and will go out of their way to do so, even if only for a moment. From Alaska to California, schools of from half a dozen to 30 or more Dall's porpoises may ride for hours in a vessel's wave, darting back and forth in front of the cleaving bow. Watching them one cannot help but enjoy their gambols and presume they must as well.

Physically, Dall's porpoise can be distinguished by its jet black color, contrasted by a large white patch on its deeply keeled flanks, and a narrow margin of white on the dorsal fin and flukes. Young Dall's porpoises (less than one year of age) have gray pigmentation where adults are white. A stranded Dall's porpoise can be distinguished from harbor porpoises by the striking black and white pigmentation and a row of 23 to 28 very small round-topped teeth in the upper and lower jaws.

Today, both harbor and Dall's porpoises suffer significantly high mortality from entanglement in fixed fishing gear (usually gillnets), presumably because they live in the nearshore environment, and their echo-location systems cannot discern the mesh. Around the San Juan Archipelago and on the outer coast of Washington, harbor porpoise carcasses occasionally wash up bearing the telltale marks of fishing nets. Although it may be too late to save the drowned porpoises, examination of the carcasses is important to absolutely determine the cause of death and examine other things, such as levels of chlorinated hydrocarbon insecticides, polychlorinated biphenyls (PCBs), and mercury, which tend to accumulate in coastal and inshore waters. Tests for these contaminants on local mammals can be useful indicators of the health of Puget Sound waters.

# Harbor Porpoise
*Phocoena phocoena*

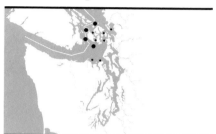

Length to 1.8 m (5.9 ft)
Weight to 72 kg (158 lbs)

**Status and Distribution**  Harbor porpoises are found in bays, harbors, and inshore waters of the temperate and boreal Northern Hemisphere. There are no good assessments of their abundance because they are too shy and unobtrusive to accurately count. Around the San Juan Archipelago there is a peak population of not more than 100 of these porpoises as best determined from aerial and vessel surveys. Harbor porpoises occur all along the outer coast of Washington State, and can sometimes be seen just outside the surf zone. In some places, such as around Peapod Rocks in Rosario Strait and near Flattop Island and Speiden Channel, a few can be found almost any time of year, suggesting that they are resident. However, small groups of them have been seen departing Haro Strait toward the Strait of Juan de Fuca and the Pacific Ocean in late fall, indicating not all are year-round residents.

As recently as the 1940s, there was a year-round population of harbor porpoises in southern Puget Sound, but now there are none. Maybe they are responding to some as yet unperceived natural cycle, increased boat traffic, or decreased food resources. It is known that dozens and dozens of them have been caught up in the mesh of gillnets and drowned, suggesting they may have been casualties that were "incidental to fisheries."

**Food and Critical Habitat**  The diet of harbor porpoises consists of small unarmored fish and invertebrates, such as herring and squids. They don't like to eat spiny creatures or fish that are larger than about one-foot long, but they have been known to take a baited fish hook.

# Dall's Porpoise
*Phocoenoides dalli*

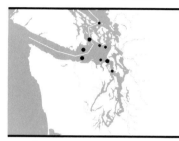

Length to 2 m (6.6 ft)
Weight to 150 kg (330 lbs)

**Status and Distribution**  Dall's porpoises are found in the temperate and boreal coastal waters of the North Pacific Ocean and in the Bering Sea, the Sea of Okhotsk, and the Sea of Japan. They are common in the Strait of Juan de Fuca and can be seen between Port Angeles and Victoria on virtually every crossing of the ferry *Coho*. In the summer they often can be seen from the Port Townsend-Keystone and Seattle-Victoria ferries cruising through Admiralty Inlet.

On rare occasions Dall's porpoises venture far into Puget Sound toward Seattle and up the Strait of Georgia toward Vancouver. In winter months and at times when prey are scarce, some remain in the area, but they are less conspicuous because they frolic less and disperse into smaller groups.

**Food and Critical Habitat**  Dall's porpoises feed on squids primarily, and on small schooling fishes if squids are not available. The preferred menu is best satisfied where there is an active turbulence and exchange of waters, such as near ocean current convergences, seamounts, and canyons, and at entrances to inshore marine waters. When feeding, this porpoise surfaces in a slow roll and arches its tail with a snappy motion as it dives. This behavior helps to distinquish it at a glance from a harbor porpoise, and earned its Indian name "broken tail."

# Mammals on the Shore

Any enumeration of the mammals of Puget Sound waters would be incomplete without some mention of the little creatures which patter along the shoreline in search of food. Raccoons eat invertebrates that reside in the intertidal zone. Meadow mice scurry around in the marshy areas consuming daily nearly their own body weight in seeds, roots, bark, and leaves. These creatures are vital to the ecology of the marshes and shores: they reduce plant material to nutrients which are replaced in the soil, and provide food for predators, such as hawks and eagles.

One shoreline creature that looks as if it is related to marine mammals is the river otter. River and sea otters are actually aquatic members of the family Mustelidae, which also includes weasels, skunks, martens, and badgers. Numerous species of river otters are found throughout the world, often ranging into estuarine habitats, and occasionally ranging into marine habitats. Invariably the "sea otters" seen in and around Puget Sound are actually river otters (*Lutra canadensis*); true sea otters (*Enhydra lutra*) are larger than river otters, and in Washington are found only on the outer coast, mostly near Cape Alava.

Nomadic in their habits, river otter families take up residence in an area while they forage for food, and move on when the preferred food species have been reduced. Occasionally, they even move in to boat houses, boats, or other shelters near water. They are not likely to be welcomed as cohabitants by people, however. Because otters are mustelids, they have musk glands and leave a distinctive acrid scent in their surroundings, which is offensive to most human noses. They are quite playful and curious, however, and are great fun to watch—unless they happen to be tearing apart your personal property in their ceaseless inquisitiveness. Their little foreflippers seem able to get into anything, followed by a flattened nose and dark curious eyes, which detect anything to eat or play with. Some river otters become so accustomed to human presence they behave like unruly pets, endlessly testing the tolerance of their human neighbors.

In some areas river otters are trapped for their pelts, which are thick and luxurious. They are not abundant, however, and can be rapidly "trapped out" of an area. Because trapping is indiscriminate, it is neither rational nor humane. The relatively small numbers that can be taken by traps in Puget Sound are not worth the risk to the local otter population. Aside from trapping there are no other major risks to the river otter populations in greater Puget Sound.

## River Otter
*Lutra canadensis*

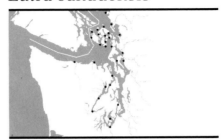

Length 1.5 m (5 ft)
Weight to 10 kg (22 lbs)

**Status and Distribution**  River otters occur throughout the Puget Sound area.

**Food and Critical Habitat**  River otters inhabit both marine and freshwater habitats of greater Puget Sound. They feed upon invertebrates, small fish, and amphibians.

*River otter near Friday Harbor*

Appendix
Bibliography
Index

# Importance of Feeding Strategy and Habitat

# Impact of Human Activity

| | Feeding Strategies | | | | | | | Nesting and Breeding Areas | | | | | | Feeding and Resting Areas | | | | | | | | Habitat Loss | | | | | | Pollution | | | | | People Pressure | | | | |
|---|---|---|---|---|---|---|---|---|---|---|---|---|---|---|---|---|---|---|---|---|---|---|---|---|---|---|---|---|---|---|---|---|---|---|---|---|---|
| | Surface-feeder | Deep Diver | Shallow Diver/Plunger | Dabbler | Stalker/Prober/Gleaner | Bird of Prey | Scavenger | Wetlands/Tidal Flats | Grasslands | Cobble/Gravel Beaches | Rocky Ledges | Soft-till Bluffs/Spoil Is. | Forests | Wetlands/Tidal Flats | Grasslands | Cobble/Gravel Beaches | Rocky Ledges | Soft-till Bluffs/Spoil Is. | Forests | Open Water | Quiet Bays | Agriculture | Industry | Dredging | Homesites | Shoreline Structures | Logging Dumps | Oil/Chem. Spill | Vessel Discharge | Industrial Discharge | Urban Discharge/Runoff | Agricultural Runoff | Vessel Traffic | Commercial Fishing | Industrial Activity | Recreational Activity | Residential Activity |
| **Marine Birds** | | | | | | | | | | | | | | | | | | | | | | | | | | | | | | | | | | | | | |
| Loons | | ● | ● | | | | | | | | | | | | | | | | | ● | ● | | | · | | | | ⬤ | ● | · | · | · | · | · | · | · | |
| Grebes | | ● | ● | | | | | | | | | | | | | | | | | ● | ● | | | · | | | ● | ⬤ | ● | ● | · | · | · | · | · | · | |
| Albatrosses | · | | | | | | | | | | | | | | | | | | | ● | | | | | | | | · | · | · | | | | | | | |
| Shearwaters | · | | | | | | | | | | | | | | | | | | | ● | | | | | | | | · | · | · | | | | | | | |
| Fulmars | · | | | | | | | | | | | | | | | | | | | ● | | | | | | | | · | · | · | | | | | | | |
| Petrels | · | | | | | | | | | · | ● | | | | | | | | | ● | | | | | | | | · | · | · | | | | | | | |
| Pelicans | · | | ● | | | | | | | | | | | | | | | | | ● | · | | | | | | | · | · | · | | | | | | | |
| Cormorants | | ● | ● | | | | | | | ● | · | | ● | | | ● | ● | | | · | · | | | | | · | · | ● | ⬤ | ● | · | ● | · | · | · | · | | |
| Herons | | | · | | ● | · | | ● | | | | | ● | | | | | ● | | · | · | ● | ⬤ | | | | | | | ● | · | ● | | | | · | · | · |
| Swans | | | | ● | | | | | | | | | | ● | ● | | | | | | ● | ● | | | · | ● | | · | ● | | | ● | | | | · | | |
| Geese/Brant | ● | | | ● | | | | | | | | | | ⬤ | ⬤ | ● | | | | | ● | ● | | ● | | · | · | · | ● | · | · | ● | · | | | · | · |
| Dabbling Ducks | ● | | | ● | · | | | ● | · | | | | | ⬤ | ● | · | | | | ● | ● | ● | ● | ● | · | · | · | · | · | · | · | ● | | ● | ● | · | |
| Bay Ducks | · | · | ● | | | | | | | | | | | | | | | | | ● | ● | | | ⬤ | | | | ● | ● | · | ● | ● | · | ● | | | |
| Sea Ducks | | ● | · | | | | | | | | | | | | | | | | | ● | ● | | | ● | | | | ● | ● | · | · | | ● | · | | | |
| Mergansers | | ● | ● | | | | | | | | | · | | | | | · | | | ● | ● | | | ● | | | | · | ● | · | · | · | ● | | · | · | |
| Eagles | ● | | | | · | ● | ● | | ⬤ | ● | | · | · | ● | ● | | · | · | · | ● | · | | | · | ● | ● | · | · | ● | | ● | · | ● | | | · | · |
| Hawks | | | | ● | | · | | | | · | | ● | | | ● | | | | · | ● | · | ● | | ● | · | · | · | ● | | · | ● | | ● | | | · | ● |
| Osprey | | | | ● | | | | | | | | ● | ● | ● | · | | | | ● | ● | | | | ● | | | · | ● | | · | ● | | | · | | · | · |
| Falcons | | | | ● | ⬤ | | | | | ● | | | | ● | · | | ● | · | ● | ● | | | ● | ● | ● | | · | ● | | | ● | ⬤ | | | | ⬤ | |
| Coots | · | | | · | · | | | | | | | | · | · | | | | | ● | | | | | | | | | | · | | | · | · | ● | |
| Oystercatchers | | | | ⬤ | | | | | · | ● | ⬤ | | ● | ⬤ | | | | | | | · | ● | · | | | | · | | · | | | · | | | | ● |
| Plovers | | | | ● | | | | | · | · | | ● | ● | · | | | | · | ● | · | ● | · | | · | | · | | · | | | · | | | · | · |
| Sandpipers | | | | ● | | | | | ⬤ | ● | · | · | | ● | | | | · | ● | · | · | ● | · | | · | | · | | ● | | · | | | · | ● |
| Phalaropes | ● | | | · | | | | | | | | | | ● | ● | | | | · | ● | · | | | | · | | | · | | | | | | | |
| Jaegers | · | | | · | ● | · | | | | | | | | ● | | | | | · | · | | | | | | | | · | | | | | | | |
| Gulls | ● | | ● | ● | · | · | ● | | | | ● | | ● | ● | ● | · | · | · | ● | ● | | · | · | · | · | · | ● | ⬤ | ● | · | · | ● | · | | · | · |
| Terns | · | | ● | | | | | | | | ● | | ● | | ⬤ | | | | ● | ● | | · | | | | · | ● | ● | · | · | · | · | · | · | · | · |
| Alcids | | ● | ● | | | | | | · | ⬤ | | | | | | ● | ● | | ● | ● | | | | · | | ● | ⬤ | · | · | · | ● | ● | ⬤ | · | · | · |
| Owls | | | | ● | | · | | | · | · | | · | | · | · | | | | · | | · | · | · | | · | | · | | | | | · | | ● |
| Kingfishers | | ● | | | | · | ● | ● | | | | | · | ● | · | | | ● | · | · | ● | | ● | ● | ● | ● | · | ● | · | · | | | |
| Ravens/Crows | | | · | · | ● | | | · | | ● | | · | ● | ⬤ | · | · | | · | | | · | · | · | | | ● | · | · | · | | | | · | |
| | | | | | | | | | | | | | | | | | | | | | | | | | | | | | | | | | | | | |
| **Marine Mammals** | | | | | | | | | | | | | | | | | | | | | | | | | | | | | | | | | | | | | |
| Harbor Seal | | | ● | | | · | | | | | ● | ● | | ⬤ | | | | | ● | | | | | | | | | | | ⬤ | · | ⬤ | ⬤ | ⬤ |
| Elephant Seal | | ⬤ | | | | | | | | | · | | | | | | | | | | | | | | | · | | | | | |
| Sea Lions | | | ● | | | | | | | | ● | | | | | | | | | | | | | | | · | · | · | · | · | · |
| Minke Whale | ● | | | | | | | | | | | | | | | | | | | | | | | | | | | | | | | |
| Gray Whale | | | ● | | | | | | | | | | ● | | | · | | | | | | · | | | | | | | | |
| Toothed Cetaceans | | ● | | | | | | | | | | | ● | | | | | | | | | | | ● | | | | | | |

Useful ·    Important ●    Critical ⬤      Moderate ·    High ●    Critical ⬤

# Annual Occurrence in Puget Sound

Symbol key — occasional = ·, common = •, very common = ◉, abundant = ●, breeding/rearing young = ▦ (gray shaded cell)

| | May | June | July | August | September | October | November | December | January | February | March | April | Notes |
|---|---|---|---|---|---|---|---|---|---|---|---|---|---|
| **Marine Birds** | | | | | | | | | | | | | |
| Loons | · | | | | · | · | • | • | • | ● | ● | • | A few red-throated loons remain through summer |
| Grebes | · | · | · | · | · | · | • | ● | ● | ● | • | • | Large winter concentrations (thousands of western grebes occur in N. Puget Sound) |
| Albatrosses | · | · | · | · | · | | | | | | | · | Black-footed albatross is an unusual visitor in the outer Strait of Juan de Fuca |
| Shearwaters | · | · | · | · | · | | | | | | | · | Rarely occur in Strait of Juan de Fuca |
| Fulmars | | | | | · | · | · | · | · | · | · | | A casual visitor to Strait of Juan de Fuca |
| Petrels | | | | | | | · | · | · | · | | | Leach's and fork-tailed petrels breed on Tatoosh Is. (May-Aug); unusual in Strait of Juan de Fuca |
| Pelicans | · | · | · | | | | | | | | | · | Brown and white pelicans are unusual visitors to Puget Sound |
| Cormorants | ▦• | ▦• | ▦• | ▦• | • | • | • | ● | ● | • | • | ▦ | All three species breed in Puget Sound or W. edge of Strait of Juan de Fuca |
| Herons | • | • | · | · | • | • | ● | ● | ● | ● | • | • | Move to salt water in large numbers as winter freezes lakes and ponds |
| Swans | | | | | · | • | • | • | • | • | · | | Whistling swans are normally found in N. Puget Sound along river estuaries in late fall and winter |
| Geese/Brant | • | | | · | • | • | ● | ● | ● | ● | ● | ● | Significant percent of West Coast snow geese and brant on Puget Sound in fall and winter |
| Dabbling Ducks | ▦• | ▦· | · | · | • | • | ● | ● | ● | ● | ● | ▦ | Mallards remain year round and breed along Puget Sound within estuaries and salt marshes |
| Bay Ducks | | | | · | • | • | ● | ● | ● | ● | • | · | A few individuals remain through breeding season with large concentrations of wintering scaup in N. Sound |
| Sea Ducks | ▦• | ▦· | ▦· | · | • | • | ● | ● | ● | ● | • | ▦ | A few remain through breeding season; harlequins breed up the major rivers |
| Mergansers | • | | | · | • | • | ● | ● | ● | ● | • | · | All three species winter and conduct courtship on Puget Sound |
| Eagles | ▦• | ▦• | ▦• | ▦• | • | • | ● | ● | ● | ● | • | ▦ | Large numbers of wintering eagles on deltas; breeding concentrations within San Juan Is. |
| Hawks | · | · | · | · | · | • | • | • | • | • | • | · | Marsh hawks winter along estuaries |
| Osprey | · | · | · | · | · | · | · | · | · | · | · | · | A few breeding pairs in N. Puget Sound and along Strait |
| Falcons | · | · | · | · | • | ● | ● | • | • | ● | ● | • | N. Puget Sound is very important to wintering and migrant peregrine falcons, with some breeding |
| Coots | | | | | · | • | • | • | · | · | • | · | |
| Oystercatchers | ▦• | ▦• | ▦• | • | • | • | • | • | • | • | • | • | Populations require isolated/undisturbed rocky beaches for reproduction |
| Plovers | ▦• | ▦· | · | · | • | • | • | · | • | · | · | ▦ | Fall and spring migrants utilize Puget Sound; killdeers breed here |
| Sandpipers | • | · | · | • | ● | ● | ● | • | • | • | · | • | Puget Sound estuaries, mudflats and beaches are very important to these species in fall and winter |
| Phalaropes | · | · | · | • | • | | | | | | | · | Northern phalaropes utilize Strait of Juan de Fuca and N. Puget Sound waters |
| Jaegers | · | | · | • | • | • | · | · | · | | | · | Parasitic jaeger normally found in N. Puget Sound in winter |
| Gulls | ▦• | ▦• | ▦• | ▦• | • | ● | ● | • | • | ● | • | ▦ | Glaucous most common; fall and winter populations of gulls are greatest |
| Terns | ▦• | ▦• | ▦• | · | • | • | • | · | | | · | • | Arctic tern breeds in small colony; migrant common tern is most numerous |
| Alcids | ● | ● | ● | ◉ | • | • | • | • | · | • | • | ▦ | Several breeding alcids in Puget Sound; Protection Island of major importance |
| Owls | · | · | · | · | · | · | · | • | • | • | • | · | A few snowy owls migrate annually to Puget Sound shorelines in fall and winter |
| Kingfishers | ▦• | ▦• | • | • | • | • | • | • | • | • | • | ▦ | Common resident and breeding bird |
| Ravens/Crows | ▦• | ▦• | • | • | • | • | • | • | • | • | • | ▦ | Common crow very successful along Puget Sound; raven retreats to more remote reaches |
| **Marine Mammals** | | | | | | | | | | | | | |
| Harbor Seal | ● | ● | ● | ● | ● | • | • | • | • | • | • | • | Resident |
| Elephant Seal | ● | | | · | • | • | • | | | | | ● | Visitors during migration |
| Sea Lions | • | | | | | | • | ● | ● | ● | ● | ● | Winter visitors |
| Minke Whale | • | · | • | ● | ● | ● | • | · | · | · | · | · | Residents and summer visitors |
| Gray Whale | • | • | ● | ● | ● | • | · | · | · | · | · | · | Visitors |
| Toothed Cetaceans | · | · | • | ● | ● | • | · | · | · | · | · | · | Resident |

Occasional ·    Common •    Very Common ◉    Abundant ●    Breeding/rearing young ▦

Presence and Distribution of Marine Animals:
# Mud and Fine Sand Beach Habitat

Occasional ● Common ● Abundant ● Breeding/rearing young ☐

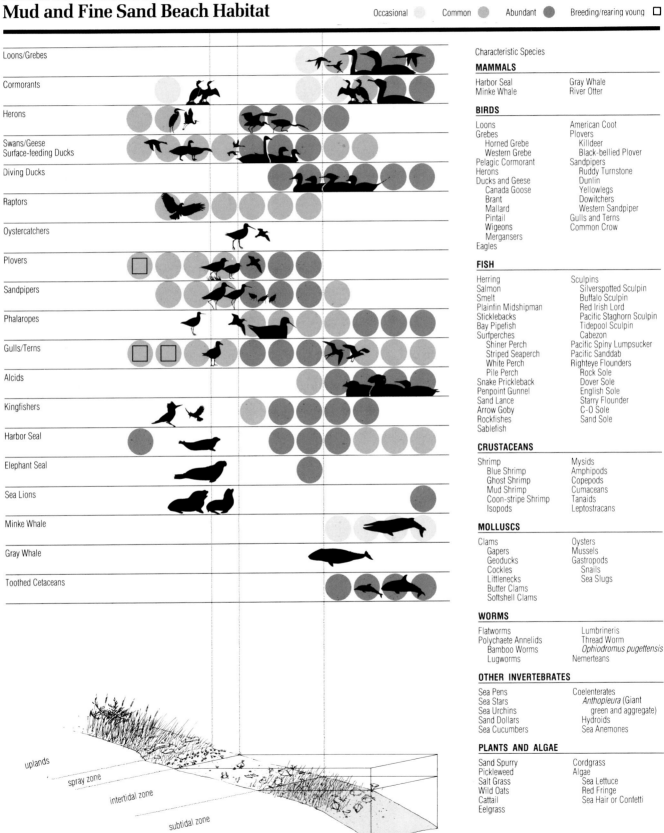

Loons/Grebes

Cormorants

Herons

Swans/Geese
Surface-feeding Ducks

Diving Ducks

Raptors

Oystercatchers

Plovers

Sandpipers

Phalaropes

Gulls/Terns

Alcids

Kingfishers

Harbor Seal

Elephant Seal

Sea Lions

Minke Whale

Gray Whale

Toothed Cetaceans

uplands

spray zone

intertidal zone

subtidal zone

Characteristic Species

## MAMMALS

| | |
|---|---|
| Harbor Seal | Gray Whale |
| Minke Whale | River Otter |

## BIRDS

| | |
|---|---|
| Loons | American Coot |
| Grebes | Plovers |
|   Horned Grebe |   Killdeer |
|   Western Grebe |   Black-bellied Plover |
| Pelagic Cormorant | Sandpipers |
| Herons |   Ruddy Turnstone |
| Ducks and Geese |   Dunlin |
|   Canada Goose |   Yellowlegs |
|   Brant |   Dowitchers |
|   Mallard |   Western Sandpiper |
|   Pintail | Gulls and Terns |
|   Wigeons | Common Crow |
|   Mergansers | |
| Eagles | |

## FISH

| | |
|---|---|
| Herring | Sculpins |
| Salmon |   Silverspotted Sculpin |
| Smelt |   Buffalo Sculpin |
| Plainfin Midshipman |   Red Irish Lord |
| Sticklebacks |   Pacific Staghorn Sculpin |
| Bay Pipefish |   Tidepool Sculpin |
| Surfperches |   Cabezon |
|   Shiner Perch | Pacific Spiny Lumpsucker |
|   Striped Seaperch | Pacific Sanddab |
|   White Perch | Righteye Flounders |
|   Pile Perch |   Rock Sole |
| Snake Prickleback |   Dover Sole |
| Penpoint Gunnel |   English Sole |
| Sand Lance |   Starry Flounder |
| Arrow Goby |   C-O Sole |
| Rockfishes |   Sand Sole |
| Sablefish | |

## CRUSTACEANS

| | |
|---|---|
| Shrimp | Mysids |
|   Blue Shrimp | Amphipods |
|   Ghost Shrimp | Copepods |
|   Mud Shrimp | Cumaceans |
|   Coon-stripe Shrimp | Tanaids |
|   Isopods | Leptostracans |

## MOLLUSCS

| | |
|---|---|
| Clams | Oysters |
|   Gapers | Mussels |
|   Geoducks | Gastropods |
|   Cockles |   Snails |
|   Littlenecks |   Sea Slugs |
|   Butter Clams | |
|   Softshell Clams | |

## WORMS

| | |
|---|---|
| Flatworms | Lumbrineris |
| Polychaete Annelids | Thread Worm |
|   Bamboo Worms | *Ophiodromus pugettensis* |
|   Lugworms | Nemerteans |

## OTHER INVERTEBRATES

| | |
|---|---|
| Sea Pens | Coelenterates |
| Sea Stars |   *Anthopleura* (Giant |
| Sea Urchins |     green and aggregate) |
| Sand Dollars | Hydroids |
| Sea Cucumbers | Sea Anemones |

## PLANTS AND ALGAE

| | |
|---|---|
| Sand Spurry | Cordgrass |
| Pickleweed | Algae |
| Salt Grass |   Sea Lettuce |
| Wild Oats |   Red Fringe |
| Cattail |   Sea Hair or Confetti |
| Eelgrass | |

Presence and Distribution of Marine Animals:
# Coarse Sand and Cobble Beach Habitat

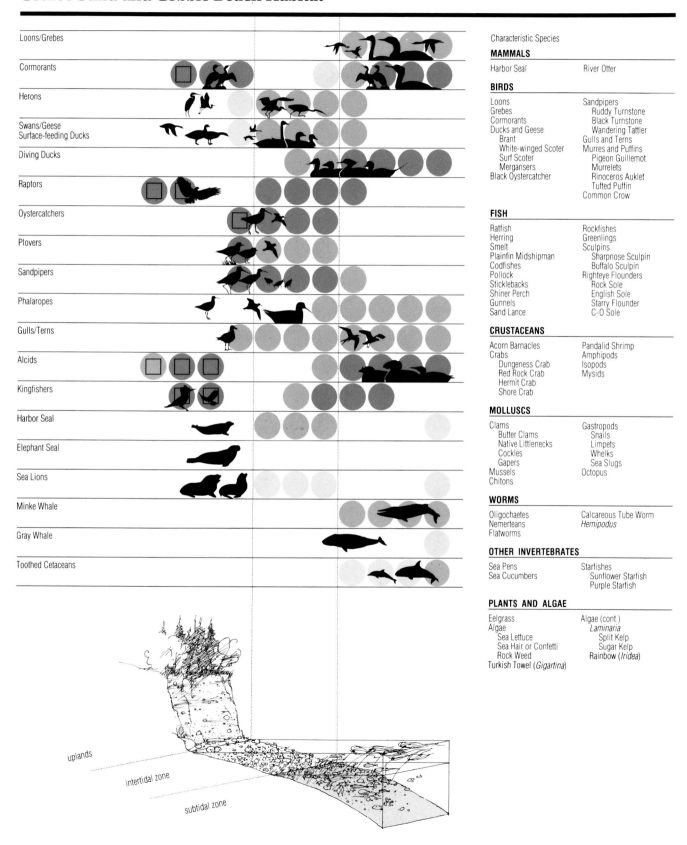

| | | |
|---|---|---|
| Loons/Grebes | | |
| Cormorants | | |
| Herons | | |
| Swans/Geese Surface-feeding Ducks | | |
| Diving Ducks | | |
| Raptors | | |
| Oystercatchers | | |
| Plovers | | |
| Sandpipers | | |
| Phalaropes | | |
| Gulls/Terns | | |
| Alcids | | |
| Kingfishers | | |
| Harbor Seal | | |
| Elephant Seal | | |
| Sea Lions | | |
| Minke Whale | | |
| Gray Whale | | |
| Toothed Cetaceans | | |

Characteristic Species

**MAMMALS**

| | |
|---|---|
| Harbor Seal | River Otter |

**BIRDS**

| | |
|---|---|
| Loons | Sandpipers |
| Grebes | Ruddy Turnstone |
| Cormorants | Black Turnstone |
| Ducks and Geese | Wandering Tattler |
| Brant | Gulls and Terns |
| White-winged Scoter | Murres and Puffins |
| Surf Scoter | Pigeon Guillemot |
| Mergansers | Murrelets |
| Black Oystercatcher | Rinoceros Auklet |
| | Tufted Puffin |
| | Common Crow |

**FISH**

| | |
|---|---|
| Ratfish | Rockfishes |
| Herring | Greenlings |
| Smelt | Sculpins |
| Plainfin Midshipman | Sharpnose Sculpin |
| Codfishes | Buffalo Sculpin |
| Pollock | Righteye Flounders |
| Sticklebacks | Rock Sole |
| Shiner Perch | English Sole |
| Gunnels | Starry Flounder |
| Sand Lance | C-O Sole |

**CRUSTACEANS**

| | |
|---|---|
| Acorn Barnacles | Pandalid Shrimp |
| Crabs | Amphipods |
| Dungeness Crab | Isopods |
| Red Rock Crab | Mysids |
| Hermit Crab | |
| Shore Crab | |

**MOLLUSCS**

| | |
|---|---|
| Clams | Gastropods |
| Butter Clams | Snails |
| Native Littlenecks | Limpets |
| Cockles | Whelks |
| Gapers | Sea Slugs |
| Mussels | Octopus |
| Chitons | |

**WORMS**

| | |
|---|---|
| Oligochaetes | Calcareous Tube Worm |
| Nemerteans | *Hemipodus* |
| Flatworms | |

**OTHER INVERTEBRATES**

| | |
|---|---|
| Sea Pens | Starfishes |
| Sea Cucumbers | Sunflower Starfish |
| | Purple Starfish |

**PLANTS AND ALGAE**

| | |
|---|---|
| Eelgrass | Algae (cont.) |
| Algae | *Laminaria* |
| Sea Lettuce | Split Kelp |
| Sea Hair or Confetti | Sugar Kelp |
| Rock Weed | Rainbow (*Iridea*) |
| Turkish Towel (*Gigartina*) | |

uplands

intertidal zone

subtidal zone

Presence and Distribution of Marine Animals:

# Rocky Shore Habitat

Occasional ⬤ Common ⬤ Abundant ⬤ Breeding/rearing young ☐

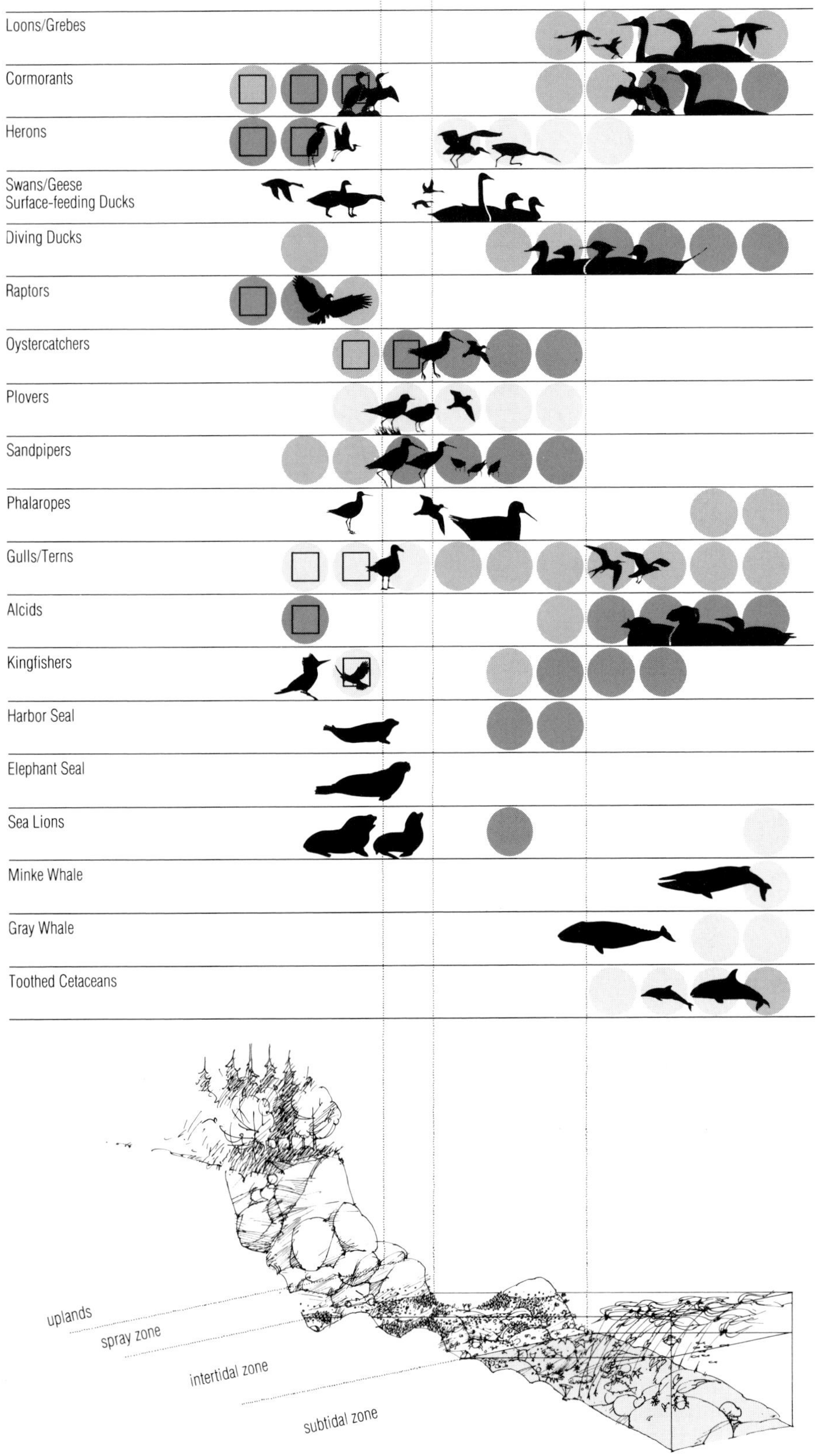

|  | | |
|---|---|---|
| Loons/Grebes | | |
| Cormorants | | |
| Herons | | |
| Swans/Geese Surface-feeding Ducks | | |
| Diving Ducks | | |
| Raptors | | |
| Oystercatchers | | |
| Plovers | | |
| Sandpipers | | |
| Phalaropes | | |
| Gulls/Terns | | |
| Alcids | | |
| Kingfishers | | |
| Harbor Seal | | |
| Elephant Seal | | |
| Sea Lions | | |
| Minke Whale | | |
| Gray Whale | | |
| Toothed Cetaceans | | |

uplands
spray zone
intertidal zone
subtidal zone

## Characteristic Species

### MAMMALS

Harbor Seal
Sea Lions

River Otter

### BIRDS

Grebes
  Red-necked Grebe
  Horned Grebe
  Western Grebe
Pelagic Cormorant
Great Blue Heron
Ducks and Geese
  Harlequin
  Surf Scoter
  Mergansers
Black Oystercatcher
Sandpipers
  Surfbird
Ruddy Turnstone

Black Turnstone
Wandering Tattler
Rock Sandpiper
Gulls and Terns
  Glaucous-winged Gull
  Western Gull
  Herring Gull
  Bonaparte's Gull
  Heermann's Gull
Murres and Puffins
  Common Murre
  Pigeon Guillemot
  Marbled Murrelet
  Auklets

### FISH

Dogfish
Ratfish
Herring
Smelt
Tomcod
Surfperches
  Striped Perch
  Pile Perch
Mosshead Warbonnet
Crescent Gunnel
Wolf-eel
Blackeye Goby
Rockfishes
  Brown Rockfish
  Copper Rockfish
  Puget Sound Rockfish
  Yellowtail Rockfish
  Quillback Rockfish

Black Rockfish
China Rockfish
Tiger Rockfish
Canary Rockfish
Yelloweye Rockfish
Greenlings
  Kelp Greenling
  White-spotted Greenling
  Lingcod
  Painted Greenling
Sculpins
  Scalyhead Sculpin
  Buffalo Sculpin
  Red Irish Lord
  Longfin Sculpin
  Great Sculpin
  Tidepool Sculpin
  Cabezon

### CRUSTACEANS

Barnacles
  Goose Barnacles
  Acorn Barnacles
Copepods
Crabs
  Decorator Crab
  Spider Crab

Sharp-nosed Crab
Red Crab
Helmet Crab
Hermit Crab
Broken-back Shrimp
Isopods

### MOLLUSCS

California Mussel
Gastropods
  Snails
  Whelks
  Limpets
Sea Slugs

Chitons
Scallops
Octopus

### WORMS

Polychaete Annelids
Flatworms

Nemerteans

### OTHER INVERTEBRATES

Sea Urchins
Sea Cucumbers
Starfishes
Brittle Stars
Sponges

Hydroids
Sea Anemones
Cup Coral
Lamp Shells
Sea Squirts

### PLANTS AND ALGAE

Lichens,
Surfgrass
Eelgrass
Algae
  *Prasiola*
  Sea Lettuce
  Green Rope

Algae (Cont.)
  Dead Man's Fingers
    or Sea Staghorn
  Rock Weed
  Bull Kelp
  Sea Moss
  Red Laver or Dulse
  Rainbow (*Iridea*)

Presence and Distribution of Marine Animals:
# Open Water Habitat

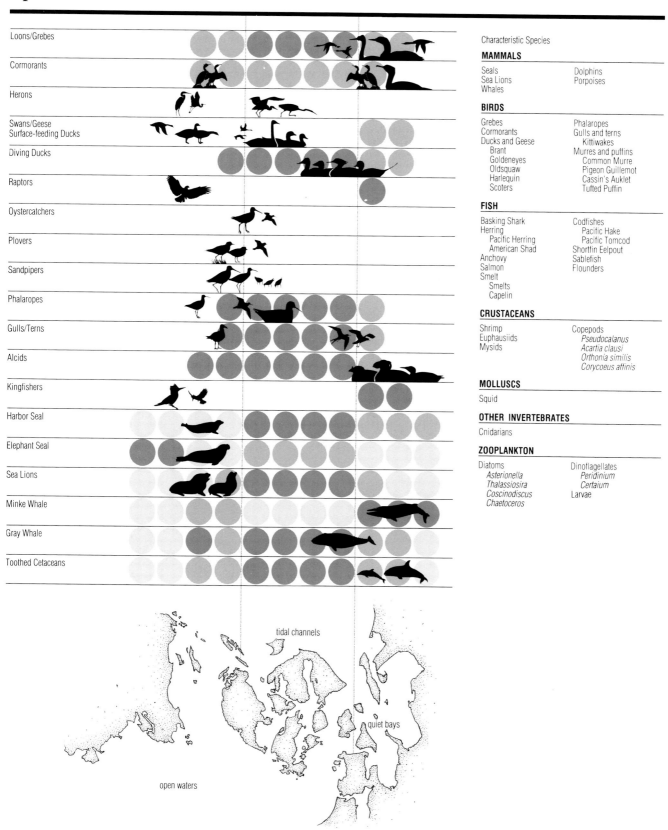

Loons/Grebes
Cormorants
Herons
Swans/Geese
Surface-feeding Ducks
Diving Ducks
Raptors
Oystercatchers
Plovers
Sandpipers
Phalaropes
Gulls/Terns
Alcids
Kingfishers
Harbor Seal
Elephant Seal
Sea Lions
Minke Whale
Gray Whale
Toothed Cetaceans

Characteristic Species

**MAMMALS**

| | |
|---|---|
| Seals | Dolphins |
| Sea Lions | Porpoises |
| Whales | |

**BIRDS**

| | |
|---|---|
| Grebes | Phalaropes |
| Cormorants | Gulls and terns |
| Ducks and Geese | Kittiwakes |
| Brant | Murres and puffins |
| Goldeneyes | Common Murre |
| Oldsquaw | Pigeon Guillemot |
| Harlequin | Cassin's Auklet |
| Scoters | Tufted Puffin |

**FISH**

| | |
|---|---|
| Basking Shark | Codfishes |
| Herring | Pacific Hake |
| Pacific Herring | Pacific Tomcod |
| American Shad | Shortfin Eelpout |
| Anchovy | Sablefish |
| Salmon | Flounders |
| Smelt | |
| Smelts | |
| Capelin | |

**CRUSTACEANS**

| | |
|---|---|
| Shrimp | Copepods |
| Euphausiids | *Pseudocalanus* |
| Mysids | *Acartia clausi* |
| | *Orthonia similis* |
| | *Corycoeus affinis* |

**MOLLUSCS**

Squid

**OTHER INVERTEBRATES**

Cnidarians

**ZOOPLANKTON**

| | |
|---|---|
| Diatoms | Dinoflagellates |
| *Asterionella* | *Peridinium* |
| *Thalassiosira* | *Certaium* |
| *Coscinodiscus* | Larvae |
| *Chaetoceros* | |

tidal channels

quiet bays

open waters

# Puget Sound and Its Approaches

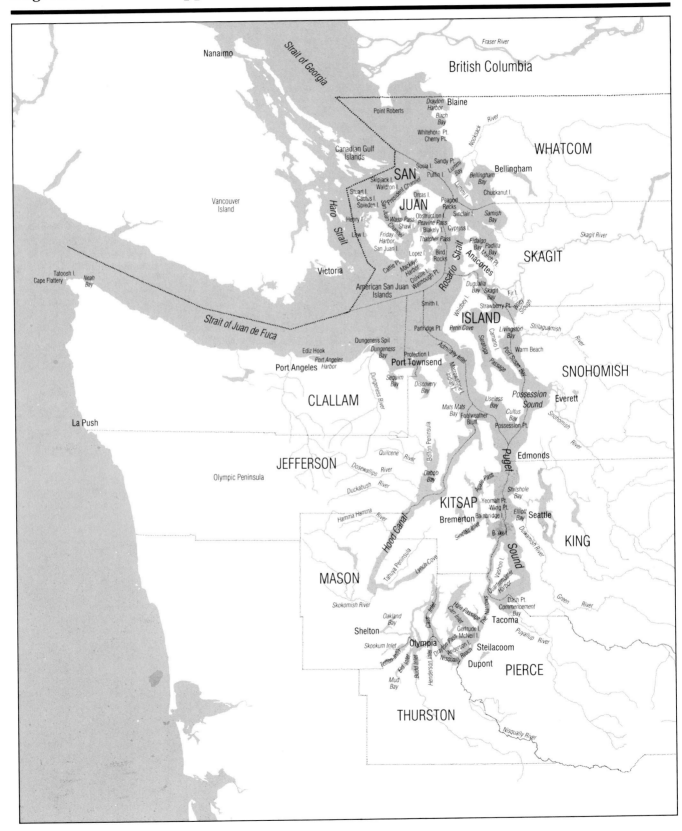

Nanaimo

Strait of Georgia

Fraser River

British Columbia

Point Roberts

Drayton Harbor  Blaine

Birch Bay

Whitehorn Pt.
Cherry Pt.

Nooksack  River

WHATCOM

Canadian Gulf Islands

Sosla I.  Sandy Pt.
Puffin I.  Lummi
Bay

Bellingham

Bellingham Bay

Chuckanut I.

SAN

Skipjack I.
Waldron I.
Stuart I.  St. President Channel
Cactus I.
Spieden I.

Orcas I.
Peapod
Rocks

Lummi I.

JUAN

Obstruction I.
Peavine Pass

Samish Bay

Vancouver Island

Haro Strait

Henry I.

Wasp Pass
Shaw I.  Blakely I.

Sinclair I.

Cypress I.

Low I.

Friday Harbor

Thatcher Pass

Fidalgo Bay  Padilla
Bay  March Pt.

Anacortes

San Juan I.

Lopez I.

Bird
Rocks

SKAGIT

Skagit River

Victoria

Cattle Pt.

Mackaye Harbor

Colville I.
Walmough Pt.

Duguella
Bay

Skagit
Bay  Fir I.  Wiley
Slough

American San Juan Islands

Smith I.

Strawberry Pt.

Tatoosh I.
Cape Flattery  Neah
Bay

Partridge Pt.

Whidbey
I.  Penn Cove

ISLAND

Livingston
Bay

Stillaguamish

River

Strait of Juan de Fuca

Camano I.

Port Susan Bay

Warm Beach

Dungeness Spit

Ediz Hook

Dungeness
Bay

Protection I.

Admiralty Inlet

Saratoga

SNOHOMISH

Port Angeles
Port Angeles  Harbor

Port Townsend

Marrowstone I.

Useless
Bay

Possession
Sound

Everett

La Push

CLALLAM

Sequim
Bay

Discovery
Bay

Mats Mats
Bay  Foulweather
Bluff

Cultus
Bay  Possession Pt.

Snohomish

River

Dungeness River

Quilcene  River

Bolton Peninsula

Puget

Edmonds

JEFFERSON

Dosewallips  River

Dabob
Bay

Shilshole
Bay

Olympic Peninsula

Duckabush  River

Agate Pass

Yeomalt Pt.
Wing Pt.
Bainbridge I.

Elliott
Bay

Seattle

Hamma Hamma  River

Hood Canal

KITSAP

Bremerton

Blake I.

Sinclair Inlet

Duwamish River

KING

MASON

Tahuya Peninsula

Lynch Cove

Sound

Vashon
I.

Quartermaster
Harbor

Dash Pt.

Green  River

Skokomish River

Oakland
Bay

Case Inlet

Hale Passage
Carr Inlet

Commencement
Bay

Tacoma

Shelton

Skookum Inlet

Olympia

Gertrude I.
Drayton Pass  McNeil I.
Anderson I.

Steilacoom

Puyallup  River

Totten Inlet
Eld Inlet
Budd Inlet

Henderson Inlet

Nisqually
Reach

Dupont

PIERCE

Mud
Bay

THURSTON

Nisqually River

# Marine Vegetation and Wildlife Areas

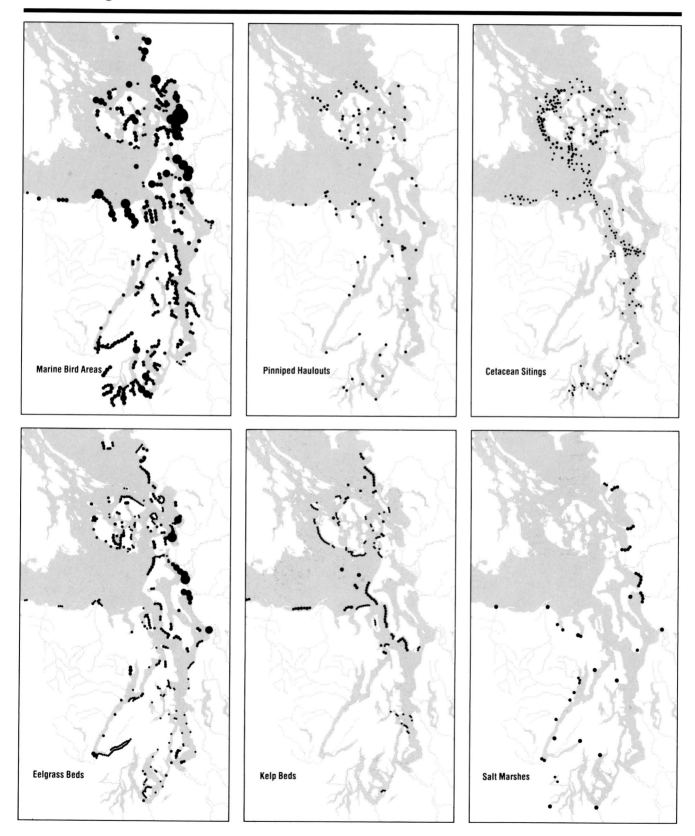

Marine Bird Areas

Pinniped Haulouts

Cetacean Sitings

Eelgrass Beds

Kelp Beds

Salt Marshes

# Marine Mammals of Puget Sound:
## Life History Notes

| | Adult Length/Weight | | Newborn Length/Weight | | Life Span | Age at Sexual Maturity | Breeding and Reproduction | Characteristic Color |
|---|---|---|---|---|---|---|---|---|
| | m | kg | m | kg | yrs. | yrs. | | |
| **Harbor Seal** | 1.8 ♂<br>1.2 ♀ | 105<br>45 | 0.8 | 10 | 30 | 6 ♂<br>6 ♀ | Monogamous; Breed in Puget Sound, July-September; Gestation 8-9 mos. delayed implantation, 2-3 mos.; 1 birth/year | Gray-brown with dark rings and spots. Dark brown at birth. |
| **Elephant Seal** | 5.0 ♂<br>3.0 ♀ | 2,000<br>800 | 1.2 | 25 | 20 | 7-10 ♂<br>3-4 ♀ | Polygynous; Breed in California-Mexico, December-February; Gestation 11 mos.; 1 birth/year | Brown. Black at birth changing to gray in first month. |
| **Northern Sea Lion** | 3.2 ♂<br>2.2 ♀ | 1,000<br>300 | 1.0 | 20 | 20 | 5 ♂<br>3-5 ♀ | Polygynous; Breed in North Pacific Islands, May-July; Gestation 11 mos. delayed implantation, 3.5 mos.; 1 birth/year | Dark brown at birth changing to tan by autumn. |
| **California Sea Lion** | 2.5 ♂<br>1.6 ♀ | 365<br>115 | 0.8 | 10 | 20 | 5 ♂<br>5 ♀ | Polygynous; Breed in California-Mexico, May-June; Gestation 11 mos.; 1 birth/year | Dark brown |
| **Minke Whale** | 9.0 ♂<br>9.0 ♀ | 9,000<br>9,000 | 2.8 | 250 | | 8 ♂<br>8 ♀ | Breed June-August; Gestation 10 mos.; 1 birth/year | Black with gray streaks, white shoulder band. |
| **Humpback Whale** | 16.0 ♂<br>16.5 ♀ | 60,000<br>62,000 | 4.3 | 800 | 30-50 | 8 ♂<br>8-9 ♀ | Breed off Hawaii and Mexico, January-February; Gestation 11 mos.; 1 birth every 2-3 years | Black with white belly, often with extensive white on flippers. |
| **Gray Whale** | 13.0 ♂<br>14.0 ♀ | 30,000<br>32,000 | 4.5 | 500 | 30-70 | 8 ♂<br>8 ♀ | Breed off Baja California, January-February; Gestation 13.5 mos.; 1 birth every 2-3 years | Gray with white and yellow patches of barnacles and whale lice |
| **Killer Whale** | 9.1 ♂<br>8.2 ♀ | 5,000<br>3,000 | 2.4 | 180 | 40 + | 8 ♂<br>8 ♀ | Breed in Puget Sound, late summer-fall; Gestation 15 mos.; 1 birth every 3 years | Black with white belly, eye patch, and flanks, and gray saddle behind dorsal fin |
| **Pacific White-sided Dolphin** | 2.2 ♂<br>2.2 ♀ | 90<br>90 | 1.2 | 25 | | 5 ♂<br>5 ♀ | Breed spring-fall; Gestation 10-12 mos. | Black with white streaks, shoulder, and belly |
| **Short-finned Pilot Whale** | 6.9 ♂<br>5.0 ♀ | 1,200<br>800 | 1.4 | | 40-50 | 12 ♂<br>6 ♀ | Breed year round; Gestation 14.5 mos.; 1 birth every 3 years | Black with grayish saddle and white patch on belly |
| **Risso's Dolphin** | 4.0 ♂<br>4.0 ♀ | 500<br>500 | | | | | Breeding/reproduction information unknown Breed in Puget Sound, late summer-fall; | Dark gray with white spots and patches |
| **Harbor Porpoise** | 1.8 ♂<br>1.8 ♀ | 72<br>72 | 0.8 | 10 | | 3-4 ♂<br>3-4 ♀ | Gestation 11 mos.; 1 birth/year | Gray to black backs with white bellies |
| **Dall's Porpoise** | 2.0 ♂<br>1.9 ♀ | 150<br>150 | 1.0 | 16 | 22 + | 8 ♂<br>7 ♀ | Breed in Puget Sound, August-September; Gestation 11 mos.; 1 birth every 3 years | Jet black with white patch on flanks |
| **River Otter** | 1.5 ♂<br>1.5 ♀ | 10<br>10 | 0.1 | 0.3 | 20 | 2 ♂<br>2 ♀ | Breed in Puget Sound, spring; Gestation 9.5-12.5 mos.; 2-4 pups in litter, 1 litter per year | Dark brown |

# References and
# Selected Bibliography

*American Birds.* 1974–1979. Christmas Bird Counts for Washington Including: Bellingham, Everett, Kitsap County, Olympia, Port Townsend, San Juan Islands, Seattle, Sequim- Dungeness and Tacoma.

American Ornithologists' Union, Committee on Classification and Nomenclature. 1982. Thirty-fourth supplement to the American Ornithologists Union check-list of North American birds. Supplement to *The Auk* 99(3). July 1982.

Angell, Tony. 1974. *Owls.* Seattle and London: University of Washington Press.

—————. 1978. *Ravens, Crows, Magpies and Jays.* Seattle and London: University of Washington Press.

Austin, Oliver. 1961. *Birds of the World.* New York: Golden Press.

Balcomb, K.C., J.R. Boran, R.W. Osborne, and N.I. Haenel. 1980. Observations of killer whales (*Orcinus orca*) in greater Puget Sound, State of Washington. Report to the Marine Mammal Commission. 23 pp.

Balcomb, K.C. and C.A. Goebel. 1976. A killer whale study in Puget Sound. Unpublished report to Marine Mammal Division, National Marine Fisheries Service final report, Contract #NA30-6-35330. Seattle, Washington. 11 pp.

Barnes, L.G. and E.D. Mitchell. 1975. Late Cenozoic Northeast Pacific focity. *Rapp. P. -V. Réun. Cons. Int. Explor. Mer* 69:34-42.

Barney, Gerald O. (Study Director) 1980. *The Global 2000 Report to the President: Entering the Twenty-first Century.* Vol. I.

Bent, Author Cleveland. 1921. *Life Histories of North American Gulls and Terns.* New York: Dover Publications.

—————. 1927. *Life Histories of North American Shorebirds, Part I.* New York: Dover Publications.

—————. 1929. *Life Histories of North American Shorebirds, Part II.* New York: Dover Publications.

Bigg, M.A. 1972. Of California sea lions on Southern Vancouver Island, British Columbia. *J. Mammalogy.*

Bigg, M.A., I.B. MacAskie, and G. Ellis. 1976. Abundance and movements of killer whales off eastern and southern Vancouver Island with comments on management. Preliminary report, Arctic Biological Station, Ste. Anne de Bellevue, Quebec. 21 pp.

Bigg, M.A. and A.A. Wolman. 1975. Live-capture killer whale (*Orcinus orca*) fishery, British Columbia and Washington, 1962-73. *J. Fish. Res. Board Canada,* 32(7):1213-1221.

Blus, L.J., B.S. Neeley, Jr., A.A. Belise, and R.M. Prouty. 1974. Orgonochlorine residues in brown pelican eggs: Relation to reproductive success. *Environmental Pollution* 7:81-91.

Bortleson, G.C., M.J. Chrzastowski, and A.K. Helgerson. 1980. *Historical changes of shoreline and wetlands at eleven major deltas in the Puget Sound region, Washington.* Hydrologic Investigations Atlas, Dept. of the Interior, U.S. Geological Survey. Atlas HA-617.

Calambokidis, J., K. Bowman, S. Carter, J. Cubbage, P. Dawson, T. Fleischner, J. Schuett-Hames, J. Skidmore, and B. Taylor. 1978. Chlorinated hydrocarbon concentrations and the ecology and behavior of harbor seals in Washington State waters. Student originated study supported by the National Science Foundation. Evergreen State College, Olympia, Washington. 121 pp.

Carefoot, Thomas. 1977. *Pacific Seashores: A Guide to Intertidal Ecology.* Seattle and London: University of Washington Press.

Cody, Martin L. 1973. Coexistence, coevolution and convergent evolution in seabird communities. *Ecology* 54:31-44.

Cooper, J.G. and Dr. G. Suckley, 1859. *The Natural History of Washington Territory.* New York: Bailliere Bros.

Couch, Aldeen B. 1966. Feeding Ecology of Four Species of Sandpipers in Western Washington. M.S. Thesis. University of Washington, Seattle.

Cox, Jeffrey M., Curtis C. Ebbesmeyer, Jonathan M. Helseth, and Carol A. Coomes. 1980. *Drift Card Observations in Northwestern Washington along Portions of Two Proposed Oil Pipeline Routes.* Seattle: Evans Hamilton, Inc. Prepared for MESA Puget Sound Project.

Dawson, Leon W. 1909. *Birds of Washington.* Seattle: Occidental Publishing Co.

Dow, D. D. 1964. Diving times of wintering water birds. *Auk* 81:556-558.

Driscoll, Andrew L. *Snohomish Estuary Wetlands Study: Basic Information and Evaluation,* Volume II. Seattle: U.S. Army Corps of Engineers.

Ehrlich, Paul R., Anne H. Ehrlich, John P. Holdren. 1977. *Ecoscience: Population, Resources, Environment.* San Francisco: W.H. Freeman and Company.

Everitt, R.D., C.H. Fiscus, and R.L. Delong. 1979. Marine mammals of Northern Puget Sound and the Strait of Juan de Fuca. NOAA Marine Ecosystem Analysis Program, Boulder, Colorado. Technical Memorandum ERL MESA-4l.

Finley, M.T. and M.P. Dieter. 1978. Toxicity of experimental iron shot versus commercial lead shot in mallards. *J. Wildlife Management* 42:32-39.

Fleming, Richard H. 1977. Time and change in Puget Sound. *The Use, Study, and Management of Puget Sound.* Seattle: Washington Sea Grant.

Fulton, Lt. J.G., 1981. U.S. Department of Transportation. Coast Guard, Washington D.C. Pollution on Puget Sound and Strait of Juan de Fuca 1975–1979. Computer printout.

Gardner, Fred, Ed. 1981. *Washington Coastal Areas of Major Biological Significance.* Olympia: Washington Department of Ecology.

—————. (Editor) 1980. *Washington Coastal Areas of Major Biological Significance,* Appendix G. Olympia: Department of Ecology.

—————. 1979 and 1978 *North Puget Sound Baseline Program 1974-1977.* Olympia: Department of Ecology.

Gilman, A.P., G.A. Fox, D.B. Peakall, S.M. Teeple, T.R. Carroll, and G.T. Haymes. 1977. Reproductive parameters and egg contamination levels of Great Lakes herring gulls. *Journal of Wildlife Management* 41:458-468.

Guiguet, C.J. 1978. *The Birds of British Columbia: Waterfowl.* Victoria: British Columbia Provincial Museum.

—————. 1978. *The Birds of British Columiba: Diving Birds and Tube-nosed Swimmers.* Victoria: British Columia Provincial Museum.

—————. 1971. *The Birds of British Columbia: Gulls,*

*Terns, Jaegers and Skua.* Victoria: British Columbia Provincial Museum.

Hartwick, E.B. 1973. Foraging Strategy of the Black Oyster-catcher. Ph.D. Thesis, University of British Columbia, Vancouver.

Hatler, David F., R. Wayne Campbell, Adrian Dorst. 1978. Birds of Pacific Rim National Park. British Columbia Provincial Museum No. 20 Occasional Paper Series.

Hesselbart, W.B. and R. Hight. 1977-79. Puget Sound aerial census: waterfowl survey and inventory. Unpublished data. Nisqually National Wildlife Refuge, U.S. Fish and Wildlife Service, Olympia, Washington.

Johnsgard, Paul A. 1979. *A Guide to North American Water-fowl.* Bloomington: Indiana University Press.

Jewett, Stanley G., Walter P. Taylor, William T. Shaw, John W. Aldrich. 1953. *Birds of Washington State.* Seattle: University of Washington Press.

Keyes, M.C. 1968. The nutrition of pinnipeds. In R. J. Harrison (ed.), *The Behavior and Physiology of Pinnipeds.* New York: Appleton-Century-Crofts. pp. 359-395.

Knight, Richard L., R.C. Friesz, G.T. Allen, P.S. Randolph. 1981. *A Summary of the Mid-winter Bald Eagle Survey in Washington.* Washington Department of Game, Olympia.

Knight, Richard L., K.E.Taylor, and J.W. Vanden Bos. 1980. *A Summary of the Mid-winter Bald Eagle Survey in Washington.* Washington Department of Game, Olympia.

Kortright, F.H. 1943. *The Ducks, Geese and Swans of North America.* Washington D.C. The American Wildlife Institute.

Kozloff, Eugene N. 1976. *Seashore Life of Puget Sound, The Strait of Georgia, and the San Juan Archipelago.* Seattle and London: University of Washington Press.

Larrison, Earl J., and Klaus G. Sonnenberg. 1968. *Washington Birds.* Seattle: Seattle Audubon Society.

Lescher, Lora L. 1974. Breeding biology of the rhinoceros auklet on Destruction Island, Washington. Small Game Management Report 1973–1974. Olympia: Washington Game Department.

Malins, Donald C. Bruce B. McCain, Donald W. Brown, Albert K. Sparks, and Harold O. Hodgins. 1980. Chemical contaminants and biological abnormalities in central and southern Puget Sound. NOAA Technical Memorandum OMPA-2. Boulder, Colorado.

Manuwal, David A., Terence R. Wahl and Steven M. Speich. 1979. *The Seasonal Distribution of Marine Bird Populations in the Strait of Juan de Fuca and Northern Puget Sound in 1978.* Seattle: Wildlife Science Group, College of Forest Resources, University of Washington.

Mathematical Sciences Northwest Inc. 1977. *Washington Coastal Areas of Major Biological Significance.* Seattle, Washington.

Mattiessenn, Peter and Ralph Palmer. 1967. *The Shorebirds of North America.* New York: Viking Press.

Miller, D.S., D.B. Peakall, and W.B. Kinter. 1978. Ingestion of crude oil; sublethal effects in herring gull chicks. *Science* 199:315-317.

Mitchell, E.D. 1966. Faunal succession of extinct North Pacific marine mammals. *Norsk Hvalfangst Tidende* 1966, no. 3, pp. 47–60.

—————. 1972. Ed., Review of biology and fisheries for smaller cetaceans. *J. Fish. Res. Board Canada* 32(7):875–1242.

Naito, Y. 1976. Harbor seal in the North Pacific. *Proc. of the Bergen Conference,* August–September 1976. Document #ACMRR/MM/SC/44.

Nash, Charlie. 1979. Personal communication.

Northern Tier Pipeline Company. Northwest Energy Company, Kitimat Pipe Line Ltd. Trans Mountain Oil Pipe Line Corporation. *Environmental Statement, Crude Oil Transportation Systems,* Volume 4, Map Addendum, Final.

Office of Financial Management. 1981. *Washington Data Book 1981.* Olympia, Washington: Office of Financial Management.

Orians, Gordon. 1980. Personal Communication.

Palmer, Ralph S. (Editor) 1976. *Handbook of North American Birds—Waterfowl* (Part 2). New Haven: Yale University Press.

—————. (Editor) 1975. *Handbook of North American Birds—Waterfowl* (Part 1). New Haven: Yale University Press.

—————. (Editor) 1962. *Handbook of North American Birds—Loons Through Flamingos.* New Haven: Yale University Press.

Parker, Richard C. and Barbara Aberle. 1977. A situation report on the *Spartina* infestation in Northwest Washington. Washington State Game Department. May 1977.

Paulson, Dennis. 1980. Personal Communications with author.

Pike, G.C. 1958. Food of the northern sea lion. Progress Reports of the Pacific Coast Stations of the Fisheries Research Board of Canada, no. 112, pp. 18-20.

Pike, G.C. and I.B. MacAskie. 1969. Marine mammals of British Columbia. Bulletin 171, Fisheries Research Board of Canada, Ottawa.

Pitelka, Frank A. 1979. *Shorebirds in Marine Environments.* Lawrence Kansas: Allen Press Inc.

Radford, K.W., R.T. Orr, and C.L. Hubbs. 1965. Re-establishment of the northern elephant seal (*Mirounga angustirostris*) off central California. *Proceedings of the California Academy of Science,* 4th Series, 32(22):601–612.

Ray, G.C. and W.G. Schevill. 1974. Feeding of a captive gray whale. *Marine Fisheries Review* 36(4):31-38.

Reilly, S.B. 1981. Population assessment and population dynamics of the California gray whale (*Eschrichtius robustus*). Doctoral dissertation. University of Washington, Seattle. 265 pp.

Rice, D.W. 1977. A list of the marine mammals of the world. NOAA Technical Report NMFS SSRF-711.

Richardson, Frank. 1961. Breeding biology of the rhinoceros auklet on Protection Island, Washington. *Condor* 63:456–473.

Robbins, Chandler S., Bertel Bruun, and Herbert S. Zim. 1966. *Birds of North America.* New York: Golden Press.

Salo, Leo J. 1975. *A Baseline Survey of Significant Marine Birds in Washington State.* Olympia: Washington State Departments of Game and Ecology.

Scammon, C.M. 1874. *The Marine Mammals of the North-western Coast of North America Together with an Account of the American Whale Fishery.* John H. Carmany and Co.; San Francisco and G.P. Putnam and Sons, New York. (Available in paperback reprint from Dover publications, Inc., New York).

Scheffer, Victor B. and John W. Slipp. 1948. The whales and dolphins of Washington State with a key to the cetaceans of the West Coast of North America. *The American Midland Naturalist* 39(2):257–337.

Scheffer, T.H. and T.C. Sperry. 1931. Food habits of the Pacific harbor seal, *Phoca vitulina richardii. J. Mammal,* 12(3):214-226.

Schmitt, F.P., C. DeJong, F.H. Winter. 1980. *Thomas Welcome Roys, America's Pioneer of Modern Whaling.* Mariner's Museum Publication No. 38. Charlottesville, VA: The University Press of Virginia, 251 pp.

Sealy, S.G. 1972. Adaptive Differences in Breeding Biology in the Marine Bird Family Alcidae. Ph.D. Thesis, University of Michigan, Ann Arbor.

Shoreline Management Act of 1971. *Revised Code of Washington,* Chapter 90.58.

Sileo, L., L. Karstad, R. Frank, M.V.H. Holdrinet, E. Addison, and H.H. Braun. 1977. Organochlorine poisoning of ring-billed gulls in southern Ontario. *Journal of Wildlife Disease* 13:313-322.

*Seattle Times.* Boaters, pilots, threaten geese in Skagit and Pt. Susan Bays. Jan. 17, 1981.

Tinbergen, Niko. 1960. The evolution of behavior of gulls. *Scientific American.* 203:118–133.

U.S. Department of Commerce. Quantification of pollutants in suspended matter from Puget Sound. NOAA Technical Memorandum. ERL MESA–49.

——————. 1974. Administration of the Marine Mammal Protection Act of 1972. Report of the Secretary of Commerce. *Federal Register,* Monday, June 24, 1974. 39(122):23896–23932.

University of Washington, Institute for Environmental Studies. 1982. Marine Sanctuary Program. *Environmental Outlook* 10(8). August 1982.

Wahl, Terence R. and Dennis Paulson. 1971. *A Guide to Bird Finding in Washington.* Seattle: University of Washington.

Washington State Department of Ecology. 1978. *Coastal Zone Atlas of Washington Vol. III: San Juan County.* Olympia.

——————. 1979. *Coastal Zone Atlas of Washington Vol. V: Snohomish County.* Olympia.

——————. 1979. *Coastal Zone Atlas of Washington Vol. X: Kitsap County.* Olympia.

——————. 1978. *Coastal Zone Atlas of Washington Vol. XI: Jefferson County.* Olympia.

——————. 1979. *Coastal Zone Atlas of Washington Vol. IV: Island County.* Olympia.

Washington State Department of Game. Job Completion Report 1976-77, Waterfowl Survey and Inventory. Olympia, Washington.

Washington State Department of Natural Resources. 1974. *Washington Marine Atlas.* Division of Marine Land Management. Olympia: Department of Natural Resources. Volumes I and II.

Weig, Allen, Ed. 1880. Northwestern Washington with detail description of the Counties of Jefferson, Clallam, Island, San Juan, and Whatcom. Facsimile reproduction, Shorey Publications.

Wetmore, Alexander. 1965. *Water, Prey and Game Birds of North America.* Washington D.C. The National Geographic Society.

*Male marsh hawk
scouting for prey*

Horned grebes in breeding plumage

# Index

*Trio of pelagic cormorants*

Other books in the Puget Sound Series

**The Water Link**
A History of Puget Sound as a Resource
Daniel Jack Chasan

**Governing Puget Sound**
Robert L. Bish

**The Coast of Puget Sound**
Its Processes and Development
John Downing

**The Fertile Fjord**
Plankton in Puget Sound
Richard M. Strickland